# HOW
# DO
# YOUR
# CHILDREN
# GROW?

Eda J. LeShan

DAVID McKAY COMPANY, INC.

NEW YORK

HOW DO YOUR CHILDREN GROW?

Copyright © 1971 by Eda J. LeShan

This book is based upon a television series of the same title conducted by Eda J. LeShan over WNET/Channel 13, New York. The program series was made possible by a special grant of the Helena Rubenstein Foundation.

LIBRARY OF CONGRESS CATALOG CARD NUMBER: 71–158065
MANUFACTURED IN THE UNITED STATES OF AMERICA

# CONTENTS

I wish to express my sincere thanks to Mrs. Sadie Hofstein, Mental Health Consultant of the Nassau County Mental Health Association for providing me with information about the many new resources for mental health education. Also my thanks to Mr. Alex Sareyan, Executive Director of The Mental Health Materials Center and to Mrs. Ann P. Booth, of *Plays for Living,* Family Service Association of America.

EDA J. LESHAN, New York

# Chapter I

## THE PERILOUS PATH OF PARENTHOOD

"Join with Me on an Adventure!"

Those were my words of greeting to the 33 people who had been selected to meet with me to talk about parenthood on television, in the series called *How Do Your Children Grow?* I repeat the invitation to all of you. I hope you can join us in the same spirit with which we met and talked together while taping the program.

The parents who discussed their children and their lives with their children on this series had all volunteered to be members of our discussion groups. I was deeply moved and inspired by their honest candor, the genuine compassion for each other, and the willingness to search for new answers, that seemed to me to come through so loud and clear. What it all came down to, was that the parents who participated in this program were willing to let all of us see their humanness —their imperfections, their uncertainties, their fears—and in this very openness they also let us see their courage and sensitivity, their dreams and hopes. It was a beautiful and inspiring experience for me to be part of their searching and growing, and I want to take this opportunity to express my love and gratitude to all of them.

Our central goal in setting up the parent discussions, was that they should be open and free to develop in whatever direction the groups wanted to move. The only controlling factor on subject matter to be covered was that the parents were divided into groups according to the age of their children. Beyond that, at no time did I say, "Tonight we will discuss such and such a subject." It was our feeling that both for participant and viewer, the opportunity to grow and to learn are greater when there are as few rules as possible, and where like life itself, one is free to respond to each new experience and feeling and idea as it comes along.

We are providing you with a list of titles at the end of each chapter which will give you an idea of at least one major theme that was discussed in each program. We also felt that you might like to have some general information about each age group that we are discussing. I have therefore prepared some background material on each age group in the form of supplementary readings from articles, television, commentaries and books that seemed appropriate.

It has also been our hope that *How Do Your Children Grow?* will be used as a springboard for other parents to get together and begin where we left off. For that purpose, I am also including resource materials that can be used for reference purposes, in meetings and discussion groups, and some background information on how such groups can be organized and led.

What we are really talking about is Parent Education; learning new ways of looking at the second most critical relationship (after marriage) each of us is likely to have during our lifetime.

*No Formulas*  I hope that no one ever gets the mistaken notion that it is possible to learn five or ten best ways to raise a child! If you are looking for final answers or some simple formulas you are doomed to disappointment! Human growth is still marvelous and mysterious and absolutely unique for each growing person. All any of us can do as parents when we listen to each other, is to try to take what we hear and absorb it in relation to who we are—what makes sense, what doesn't, what gives us a new thought or two to work on, in following our own path.

Every single child who is born is different from every other child. Each of us are only ourselves and nobody else. Life changes every day. Moods, ideas, customs change. I am not at all frightened by the ordinary, human mistakes that parents make with their children—which happen just because they are human, and complicated. Losing one's temper, changing one's mind, being inconsistent, acting out of annoyance or fatigue, doing or saying something that a child may misinterpret—all these can be changed and dealt with. What absolutely drives me up the wall is the new breed of psychologists who are telling parents that there *are* formulas for child-raising. These psychologists, called Behaviorists, have their roots back with Pavlov and his salivating dogs. They believe in conditioning—that people can be made to behave in certain ways by conditioned responses.

They are right about white rats; it works very well on them; it also works on people for short periods of time, but thus far, much to my relief and delight, conditioning does not have lasting effects and sooner or later the marvelous unpredictability of human beings comes through again.

If you want lessons in punishment-reward systems, if you want a well-written script on how and what to say to your children, you won't find it here. What we will be doing is struggling together to search out our own best feelings and ideas, our most creative and imaginative and sensitive ways of Being in the world, of realizing our best selves.

If it's recipes you want, please watch Julia Child!

* *It's So Different These Days*  One of our most difficult problems as parents is that we have been trying to do many things that don't "come naturally." New approaches to raising children have come about so rapidly that by the time our children came along we were trying to use methods that we hadn't experienced ourselves.

A father told me this story: One evening, when his daughter was a little over two years old, he had suggested in a quiet

* From *How to Survive Parenthood*. Pages 3–13, line 7.

and friendly tone that Julie bring him her pajamas so he could help her get ready for bed. Julie looked up at him with a glint in her eye and said, "I will *not,* you big dope!" He said that for a moment he felt faint and nauseous. His heart started beating faster, and his hand was shaking as he reached for a cigarette. He couldn't understand what was happening to him; he had heard about two-year-olds getting negative, and he had heard about children trying to get a rise out of their parents, and he had been told that it was normal for children to talk back as a way of proving they were growing up. Why this terrible feeling of danger and unease? He tried to understand: "I had read all the books, I knew she was just 'testing,' experimenting with her own power. And yet I felt sick, I wanted to murder her!" His wife, who had noticed her husband's shaking hand, asked, "What would have happened to you if you had ever talked to your parents that way?" Without a moment's hesitation he replied, "At the very least, I would have been struck dead by lightning."

In trying to be the reasonable, understanding modern parent, he was battling against all his own deep and half-forgotten childhood instincts. Reading books about the normality of aggressiveness in children didn't quite counterbalance those feelings and memories.

He was also taking a lot on faith. He had been raised differently; how could he be sure the new way was better? Was there any real proof? There were lots of different opinions in the new books on child-raising. How could you tell who was right—if anybody was?

I have been impressed by the parents who struggle to do things differently, to give their children experiences they never had themselves; mothers who were themselves rigidly and punitively toilet-trained at six months, trying desperately to be permissive and relaxed with a two-year-old still in diapers; mothers who were overstuffed as children, valiantly trying to listen to their pediatrician's advice that three-year-old children require very little food. I have talked to fathers who

4

"got the strap" when they were fresh or naughty, now trying to control their wish to dominate, and to use other methods, such as reasoning or isolating a child, or responding with understanding instead of threats.

Sometimes, because what we have tried to do is so strange and new, we take ourselves too seriously, and try much too hard. In trying to help their children to be less frightened of their feelings, parents often become more afraid of their own feelings! What we haven't said often enough or clearly enough is that if recognizing and accepting feelings is good for children, it's also good for their parents! If acceptance of imperfection, of human frailty, of human failings can help children to be more relaxed and to like themselves better, then this is equally true for adults.

I remember a mother I met at a nursery school meeting who came up to me after everyone else had left, and told me she just had to unburden herself; she had done something really unforgivable to her children. The past winter had been a very trying one: her daughter was three and her son four and a half, and since this had been his first year in close contact with other children, he caught one cold and childhood disease after another and passed them along to his little sister. As a result, and in combination with very bad weather, Mama had been stuck indoors with her two darling children for most of several months. She went on, "Then, one day about a week ago, when they were both still convalescing, I reached the end of my rope. They were crying and cranky and fighting with each other, and I think I went sort of crazy. I was shaking all over. I was afraid I might kill them. Even though they hadn't been out for weeks and there was snow on the ground, I put on their snowsuits and sent them outdoors. I told them they couldn't come back in until I let them. I locked the front and back doors! Then I sat down in the kitchen with a cup of coffee and the paper, and after about fifteen minutes I stopped shaking and began to calm down. Even after they started yelling I would not let them in. I stayed alone for al-

5

most an hour, and then I opened the door. I was so ashamed of myself that I never even told my husband what I did. Do you think I did them some permanent damage?" I asked about the children. Did they have a relapse, did they seem upset? No, they were well now, and they had had a good lunch and nap after they came in. They seemed a little quiet and looked at her a little warily, but nothing else had happened. Did the older child seem at all fearful later? Oh no, he could hardly wait to go back to nursery school. If the children had cried or called for help, would she have let them in? *Of course*.

I started to laugh and soon this mother laughed too. At first she was quite startled by my reaction, but pretty soon she relaxed and joined me in seeing the funny side of this scene. I told her it would be a good story to tell her children when they had children of their own. I also told her that rather than being an unnatural and evil mother she was just exactly like all the rest of us, and that I hoped she'd enjoyed her stolen moment. We sometimes reach a point where we have to be selfish and think of ourselves. Apparently her children had taken her need to be alone just for what it was: not total rejection, but human harassment and a need for relief.

*Discipline: Too Much or Too Little*   Being an adult parent involves some very thoughtful explorations of the question of discipline: what it is, what it means, what it should be. Extreme positions have been recommended in rapid succession, and parents have frequently been warned of dire consequences if they do not administer the "correct" discipline. For a long period of time we were scared to death to admit that we ever spanked our children; then it was all right if you did it calmly; then it was only all right if it was done in the heat of anger! Now, with the problems of society becoming more and more complex and our anxieties increasing about how to solve all our problems, we seem to return again to

6

looking for the simplest solution such as "back to the woodshed"—"let's beat the little b——."

One of the revolutionary concepts of our generation has been that anger and hostility are normal and natural parts of being human, and that rebelliousness in our children is important for growth. We have been trying to accept the new idea that human beings have frequently paid a high price for keeping their less lovely feelings as secret as possible; that when it was considered evil or immoral or bad to feel hate or anger, people tried to keep it inside themselves and this interfered with their fullest development. Their feelings of guilt were frequently a major factor in serious emotional disturbances: guilt could cause severe anxiety, depression, flight from reality, and an inability to work or relate to other people. Sometimes it could lead to such a blocking-off of feeling that people became too passive to be able to compete or work effectively. Sometimes anger got turned in on itself and could cause serious physical illnesses. In children, too much repression of anger could lead to learning problems, excessive fears and nightmares, stuttering, etc. Too much repression certainly seemed to play an important role in serious emotional problems.

I remember very vividly an experience I had more than twenty years ago when I was the director of a nursery school in Chicago. A Viennese doctor and his wife, refugees from Nazism, had a little boy of four attending the nursery school. They were very cultured, sophisticated people, and as I got to know them, I found that they seemed to set awfully high standards for their children, and were very strict and uncompromising in their discipline. When the mother came to school for a conference with me, she was full of complaints about Peter—he was naughty, disrespectful and defiant. I tried to explain how in America we were trying to understand young children, recognize their feelings and learn from their behavior. We talked about the fact that we had learned that all children, all people, have angry feelings, and that if we

7

bottle them up completely we may create so much guilt that emotional difficulties of a serious nature may follow. She told me that her elderly mother, who was living with them, was very partial to Peter's younger brother, and while Peter controlled his feelings when he was with his grandmother, he expressed his unhappiness and jealousy toward his mother instead. She began to see that Peter's feelings made a lot of sense, but she was still afraid of permitting him to be "fresh and disrespectful." Everything in her own childhood spoke out against such behavior.

One Sunday afternoon my husband and I were invited to a Viennese *Kaffeeklatsch* at their home, where we met many of their friends, also refugees to this country. During the afternoon Peter, his younger brother and his grandmother came in from the park. Peter was scowling and looked ready to explode. His mother asked him to go upstairs and get washed up, and then come and meet the guests. Peter screamed at her, "Shut up! I don't want to—I hate you!" A deadly hush fell on the guests for a moment, followed by a heated discussion during which most of the guests warned the parents that if they permitted such behavior, Peter would become an "American delinquent, just like all those terrible children you read about in the newspapers." This bombardment went on for some time, and the mother seemed more and more embarrassed and uncomfortable, and finally, losing her temper, she said, "It seems to me you have all forgotten why you are in this country; better Peter should let me know *now* when he is angry than he should keep it all inside of him until it grows bigger and bigger and he gets so angry, he wants to put people in gas chambers!"

Another major consideration in the development of a point of view opposed to repression was that people could become not only emotionally ill or socially destructive, but they could also turn anger towards themselves and become physically sick; the development of psychosomatic medicine did, and still does suggest that physiological, biochemical changes can

8

take place under strain and tension of unacknowledged, repressed feelings. Changes in ideas about discipline do not seem so illogical if we recognize that repressive controls can lead to severe illnesses such as asthma, ulcers, migraine headaches and many other serious medical problems. This field of research is still very young, and we certainly don't know just how or when there is an interaction between psyche and soma. But we *can* say that while much of the complexity of mind-body is still a mystery to us, there is overwhelming evidence that the strain of repression and guilt plays a part in much physical illness.

We have learned that there is just no such thing as a good person or a bad person; each of us are "God and Devil," angel and animal, with the capacity for being loving and good, and with an equal capacity for being primitive and animalistic. Furthermore, we *need* both sides. Much of our vitality, creativity, drive, ambition, and healthy rebelliousness, is related to what is instinctual in us and may be expressed in curiosity, humor, the capacity to endure, and the willingness to fight for principle. If we were all sweetness and light, half the vitality of being human would disappear!

Educational exploration was moving in a similar direction. John Dewey and the other early leaders of the progressive education movement said that if we wanted children to think for themselves, if we wanted them to be civilized human beings, we had to help them develop inner controls. We can't just make them behave out of fear; then they will always need strong police authority to control them. We would have to try to help children learn to live responsibly and constructively with each other, by example, through love and understanding. It was a highly idealistic philosophy and does not deserve the criticism or blame frequently heaped upon it. As in all new areas of exploration, its only crime was oversimplification. The goals were noble, but not enough was known about human limitations and the slow way in which children get ready for self-control.

9

With our new attitude towards discipline, we began to see that behavior was highly significant: when a child did something that we felt was naughty or that seemed incomprehensible to us, he was really telling us something important about himself, and we could learn how to help him if we tried to understand instead of just punishing or stopping the behavior.

A child expert wrote in a book in the forties that if a young child became destructive of property after the birth of a brother or sister, we should understand that his natural jealousy is being exposed in this way. She recommended that we say, "That's all right Johnny, I know you smashed that lamp because you are really angry at us for bringing a new baby home." At the beginning of our new knowledge we were confused about the difference between understanding behavior, accepting the existence of undesirable feelings, and permitting expression of those feelings. It was again an understandable error that we are learning to correct. Feelings can be understood and accepted without our forgetting that there must also be controls on behavior.

But it *was* intriguing—this game of finding the hidden meanings! Kenny was in a nursery group of mine many years ago. He was a very bright and active little boy, with lots of charm, a natural leader in the group. When his mother had a baby, he seemed to go to pieces in nursery school; he would come in looking sad and withdrawn, refuse to take his coat off, sit under a table sucking his thumb and refuse to play all morning. When we called his home, his mother was shocked; nothing like that was going on at home; he loved the baby, wanted to hold her and feed her, and help with the bath. He hadn't shown any signs of jealousy at all.

I was getting nowhere with Kenny in school; the same behavior went on day after day. Finally I decided to take a chance—I had nothing to lose, and if I was wrong . . . well, Kenny would just think I was nuts! I got under the table with him and whispered, "I know lots of little boys who

10

don't like it when they get a new baby. It makes them very sad. It's okay to be mad—you won't do anything bad." Kenny looked at me in horror, ran for the closet and sat in his cubby, more remote than ever, and I figured I had really made a worse mess of things, after all. Just before it was time to go home, however, Kenny came over to me and said he had a secret to tell me. He led me to the darkest corner of the closet and whispered in my ear, very softly, "I *do* hate her and she's going to die." We had a little chat about how angry feelings could *never* make a bad thing happen, and that everyone had angry feelings, but that this didn't mean they had to do angry things about it.

I was puzzled as to why Kenny had reacted more strongly than most other children, and I thought I ought to talk to his mother. I went to see her, and when I repeated Kenny's comment she began to cry. She then told me that when Kenny was two and a half she had had another baby girl, who had only lived for six weeks. She didn't think Kenny had been old enough to understand anything about it, and since he never asked what had happened to the baby, they never gave his any explanation. How terribly frightened Kenny must have been that his bad thoughts could *again* make a baby disappear!

This story has always epitomized for me why the experts spoke against the bottling up of feelings, the dangers of repression, the importance of finding a meaning of behavior. In many ways they were on the right track, and we learned to respond more meaningfully and logically to such problems as Kenny's. I remember another day when a friend took me and his five-year-old son to visit a children's camp where he had been the director the summer before. When we got there swarms of children climbed all over him in delight and with great affection. He told a group of them a story, and spent most of the afternoon surrounded by his devoted admirers. His son, David, followed in the rear, watching. Toward suppertime David seemed to go berserk; he knocked over a

11

pitcher of milk, he hit an innocent bystander with a rubber-tire swing, he marched up and down the benches in the dining room and refused to sit down and eat. Suddenly his father looked very thoughtful, and stopping himself in the middle of shouting and threatening, he gathered David into his arms, rocked him like a baby and said, "David, you poor boy—did you think I forgot you? Do you think I love these boys and girls the way I love you? I'm just visiting some friends, but you're my *son*."

This seems to me to be one of the best ways in which understanding influenced discipline. This was a wise and conscientious and compassionate act, and the only thing wrong with it was that a lot of us assumed that this sort of thing would take care of *everything* and children would grow up without any problems if we could handle them this way. First of all, none of us could be that good all the time; many times we are tired, impatient, and can't understand at all. Sometimes we embarrass our children by understanding too much, and they lose a much-needed privacy to feel without being exposed. Understanding also doesn't change our basic personalities or our own problems, in work or marriage. Some parts of life are painful; we can't always get away from it, and it isn't always good to try. Some of these children who were "understood" and kept as frustration-free as we could manage, whom we treated with kid gloves so "God forbid, they shouldn't catch a trauma," are now young adults, and too many of them still can't take frustration or discomfort, and can't postpone an immediate need or wish, or practice any self-control; they want what they want when they want it.

Permissiveness often grew out of loving concern. It was not weak-minded or lazy in its origins. Disenchantment began to set in, however. Educators found that example and logic were not turning young savages into civilized human beings—all controls could not be internalized during the early years of childhood—and in fact all of us, adults and children, would always need external social controls in some areas.

We began to see that accepting feeling and having a more

12

realistic view of human beings did not necessarily mean permitting a child to say anything he wanted, any more than it meant letting him do whatever he felt like doing. We began to say instead, "I know you're angry, but you may not talk to me that way. It hurts my feelings and it is unkind. Go be mad alone, or tell me what's on your mind in a pleasanter way."

The dinosaurs among the older generation who can't understand why young people might be out of their heads over the state of the nation, have come up with the reassuring (to them) notion that once upon a time, Dr. Spock brainwashed every American parent into permissively raising a generation of brats. Neither Dr. Spock nor any of the rest of us ever recommended abdication from parental responsibility. Any parent who permissively allowed his child to become an animal did so without our blessing. The large majority of parents who were influenced by the new ideas about discipline were concerned with freeing their children to grow better, not wilder, and if they were less punitive and authoritarian in their discipline, their goal was to make their children more independent and compassionate.

Children who were raised by this kind of approach have problems, of course. Life is very complicated, people react differently to similar experiences, we needed to learn modifications that were useful with different kinds of children. Parental imperfections made it impossible to be consistent, parents being human beings, whatever you may have heard to the contrary! No matter how noble our motives and goals, we are often short-tempered, less than reasonable, impatient, tired and inconsistent. The complexities of the world around us—the rapidity of change, the increasing mobility and anonymity of crowded urban life, the terrible dangers, the enormous changes in the nature of work, in family life—all of this has affected our children. But with all of these modifying influences it seems to me we still have valid and clear evidence that giving children what they need, is a sensible, responsible approach to discipline and does not cause their

13

ruination. Quite the contrary; the large majority turned out to be idealistic and courageous young adults.

* Discipline is a tool that expresses our point of view about civilized living. No parent can or should be expected to sit down and contemplate, "Now, how shall I respond to this?" every time a child misbehaves. It is just this self-consciousness which has made us anxious and unspontaneous and therefore unhuman with our children. But we *can*, in some quiet and peaceful moment, over morning coffee after the children have gone to school, or over a bedtime snack after they've gone to sleep, decide what we believe discipline is in principle. The more we really think about it and incorporate our thoughts and feelings, the more we will be able to respond sensibly, without thinking, when we need to.

But how do we pin that down to practical living? Well, for me it means that, being human, I will often make mistakes; I will be unfair or impatient; I may be more severe one day than another, depending on my own mood. What can I do about it? I can try to make amends; I can say, "I'm sorry."

At a morning discussion meeting, one mother arrived looking shaken and miserable. She said that for months she had been trying to find some way to make her ten-year-old daughter stop dawdling. She had been late to school three times, and the mother had tried threats, nagging, yelling, bribes, sweetness and patience—nothing made any difference. No matter what time she woke Laurie up, the child managed to get behind schedule. On this particular morning, because she was trying to get out of the house herself to attend the meeting, she was more impatient and annoyed than usual. She told us, "I just got so mad when I saw her sitting on her bed daydreaming—when I thought she was already dressed—that I gave her the worst bawling-out of her life. Before I knew what I was saying, I yelled, 'And I'm cancelling your birthday party for Saturday—you can just tell your friends why, too! You are a selfish, inconsiderate brat and I'm not

* From *How to Survive Parenthood*. Pages 14–19, line 23.
14

going to work to give you a party when you don't care how you treat me!" Laurie was so shocked that she just gasped, and then she began to cry as if her heart would break. I didn't know what to do. I wasn't thinking when I said it— I really don't want to punish her so severely—I was just having a temper tantrum of my own. How can I expect her to un-invite her guests? But what kind of discipline can I maintain if I give in and don't carry through?"

We all agreed she could have the very *best* of discipline, the kind that says, "I went too far, I made a mistake—I'm big enough to say so—forgive me." That didn't mean a whitewash of Laurie's responsibility for getting to school on time. That must still be worked at, of course. But the discipline that sets an example for maturity and civilized relationships is the best kind there is.

Authority is essential. It provides a restrictive but secure outer world with clear-cut standards and necessary controls. We have all seen the relief and relaxation in our children's faces when they know we care enough to be policemen when we have to. As far as we can tell, children and adults alike will never be able to have all of life controlled from within; we all need a certain amount of social enforcement of necessary controls. To have the courage and energy to insist on certain basic standards is much more a sign of love than giving in—which is easy. It's *not* giving in that is hard—and our children know that very well!

One night we were visiting some friends who began to reminisce about their honeymoon trip. Their nine-year-old daughter was enthralled with the story. Her mother said it was a shame: they had had wonderful pictures of their trip but Kathy had torn them all up when she was about three years old. "Why did you let me do it?" wailed Kathy, and her mother replied in all honesty, "Because I didn't know any better."

*Fostering Independence*   At the same time that we recognize our obligations to act like grown-ups about important

15

issues, we also have to give children permission to rebel; it is a necessary part of cultivating judgement and being able to function independently. I sometimes marvel at the wonderful force in children which seems to urge them on even in the face of great danger! They will suffer parental disapproval, anger, punishment, even the loss of love, in order to insist on growing up! Rebellion is really an act of integrity—it is a refusal to remain passive and dependent.

When you think about it, wouldn't it really be much easier for a child to let you make all his decisions, and do everything for him? It is really quite comfortable and pleasant, not having to worry about anything! Compared to the comfortable safety of staying at home, why does any child want to go to nursery school—a jungle of other children who may hit him or not like him; why does he want to walk to school alone—he's got to watch for the light and he may be ambushed by a big bully two grades higher up. Look at the havoc he creates when he starts to say *no!* People get madder than they've ever been before, all sorts of unpleasant things begin to happen. Rebellion is a kind of muscle-flexing. And at each stage of growth we have to figure out how much rebellion to tolerate—how much is possible, safe, endurable.

Tolerance to rebellion also means being able to endure some expression of open anger and some rough and open warfare. After his mother had lost her temper and shouted at Peter, "Just stop using that tone with me," her son replied. "First of all, you're using 'that tone' too, and secondly, if I can't yell here, where *can* I yell?"

We are learning that it is not necessary to permit children (or ourselves!) to be completely uncontrolled in how we express our feelings, even verbally, but at the same time, life will be much easier if we don't take occasional flare-ups too seriously.

*No Peas in a Pod*  Children are as unlike each other in personality as in their fingerprints. I suspect that this single factor accounts for more of our troubles than anything else. There are some babies who are angelic and who grow up so easy to raise we hardly know they're around. And then there are those others, at the other end of the scale, who, no matter what you do, are going to be screaming and fighting their way through life, manufacturing troubles if none are at hand.

The early research on children was enormously important. It was a necessary step, and it was carried on by able, imaginative and dedicated people. But its effect on parents was very strong and has, in some ways, led to our present feeling of dismay. When a theory tends to bring all children together, it suggests very strongly that what makes for differences are not internal forces within the child, but the variations in the environment. Much of the guilt, anxiety and uncertainty of many of today's parents lies in the fact that for twenty-five to fifty years they have been told that *handling* makes the crucial difference.

By studying children very intensively from birth on up through grade school and adolescent years, today's researchers are finding that children have unique and entirely individual styles, ways of coping with the environment, and that differences in ways of mastering challenges are normal, healthy and need to be understood and respected.

This may sound like a calm and sensible statement, but for those of us who have lived through the "era of environment," it is quite a change. I was married and became a parent during a time when I believed, along with most of the other "enlightened modern parents" around me, that the environment I created would decide exactly what my child would be like. If I was patient and understanding, she would be loving and good; if I fed her on self-demand, she would be secure and happy. If I handled each stage well, a predictable picture was going to be very positive. I recently met a friend who was reminiscing about her college days and the course she had taken in child psychology. We were taught that what happened to children was caused by parents. What

17

a terrible burden this has been, and how illogical and untrue it now seems! This kind of thinking did a great deal of damage. It made parenthood a contest, a nightmare of fear, and it also caused us to guiltily overindulge our children because at times we really hated them for proving our imperfections and for taking up so much of our time doing it!

Wiser parents, who somehow maintained their sanity during all this madness, knew perfectly well that their children were very rarely alike, and that they could see these differences at birth; that while one baby nursed happily and quietly and then slept like an old rag doll, another baby was colicky and tense, fighting and yelling and jerking. One child would have an optimistic view that life would be comfortable with himself and others, while another started to fight for survival against the enemy at birth. And just as children seem to have a style or a unique quality, parents seem to react to these different types, to have strong likes and dislikes, and to know intuitively that one type or another is easy or hard for them to raise; we are constitutional types too, by golly!

The important element in this view of children is that it suggests very strongly that while the environment influences a child's life experience, it can only work with the constitutional qualities the child presents. For example, it is easy to see why encouraging all parents to use demand-feeding with newborn babies couldn't work successfully for all babies. Those with a steady inner rhythm would react beautifully; those with no such inner rhythm would not be able to establish their own pattern, might get over tired and begin to cry. Mother might think he was hungry and because he was not, he might get colicky. The baby would be as confused as everyone around him. This kind of a baby might have been much happier in the era of strict schedules, because he needs to be provided with some external structure to his life.

We cannot change the basic nature or constitutional differences in children; but if we watch for the emerging patterns, if we get some sense of the natural tendencies and consis-

18

tencies in a child's responses, we can help him to live happily within that framework. For example, if Jimmy is the type of child who must have a chance to look things over before getting involved, it makes a great deal of difference if his parents accept or reject this need. If Jimmy is made to feel ashamed because he hesitates and holds back, this sense of failure will affect other aspects of his growth. If Jimmy is accepted as a perfectly nice little boy who needs to take his time, and who does just fine if you let him meet new situations in his own way, his self-confidence is bolstered. An active child who reacts with great sensitivity to everything that is going on around him will react differently to stressful situations than a more placid and less reactive child.

The new research on child development . . . offers a constitutional amendment to parents which is as liberating as the Emancipation Proclamation. Our children, it seems, are not putty in our hands! Perhaps now, freed of the heavy weight of culpability and guilt, we will be able to use our good sense and good will, to accept our children as they are, and provide an environment that measures itself in terms of differences. Being less fraught with anxiety we may be able to accept what can't be changed, and change what can be changed.

*Seeing Yourself in Your Child*  We were having a conference at the nursery school, and the mother sitting opposite me was saying, "Tracy is stubborn and strong willed and one of these days I may kill her." Then she added, not at all to my surprise, "Of course she's just like me."

Over and over again this theme seems to be repeated—the great oversensitivity to likenesses between parent and child. One probable reason for this is that very few people seem to grow up really liking themselves. It seems to be the nature of things that what our parents found difficult to handle in us we came to view as handicaps, when in truth, these may have

* From *Natural Parenthood*. Pages 19–24.

been some of our more important qualities. It is hard to handle a noisy, obstreperous kid with a mind of his own; it is hard to raise a child who desperately wants to be independent. It is nervewracking to have a child who is so curious and daring and adventurous that he gets himself into one scrape after another. And as any parent can tell you, it is harder to raise a creative, sensitive child than a placid, stolid type. And yet all of these deplored qualities may become the sources of unique strength in adulthood. However, by that time, we have usually accepted our parents' distress as a judgment, and self-contempt and self-hatred are common feelings.

Then, when one's child turns out to have the same tendencies, we are really in a bind. How can we bear to let a child have the same qualities that bug us about ourselves? We identify our child's characteristic with our discomfort and unhappiness as children, and every indication of similarity between us is salt in a raw wound.

That's one kind of over identification with our children that may make their growing more difficult. Another kind is where we cannot endure their frustrations and pain. *They* may have the strength and toughness to endure those ordinary stresses that are part of living and growing, but we cannot bear it because we are over involved. The mother who recalls the agonies of being a wallflower at her first dance falls apart when her teen-age daughter isn't asked to the school prom by the boy of her choice; a quiet, introverted father finds it unendurable when his son can't fight back when he's picked on by the school bully. Our children, who may have none of our anguish about these issues, are surviving quite well—are nowhere nearly as upset as we are—but old wounds make us more susceptible and twice as vulnerable.

Another over-identification hang-up is when we need our children to live out our dreams—where, in one way or another, there has not been enough fulfillment in our own

20

lives. A sense of emptiness make us revel in their good grades; a lack of focus in our lives makes us dream of some professional success for a child who as yet hasn't a thought in his nicely normal head other than the next baseball game; we curdle at his penmanship at nine—how can he ever be that judge or senator we dream of? When a parent's life is barren and unfulfilled each triumph seems to be his instead of his child's. Such over identification with a child's successes can interfere with his right to his own growing as much as identifying with his setbacks and failures. Whenever you succeed at something just to please a parent rather than yourself, a kind of impurity comes into the struggle.

Loving and letting go doesn't start in adolescence. It really starts at two and three when parents must make the first step in letting a child become *himself,* with no strings attached. A child cannot carry the burden of old hurts, unfulfilled dreams, feelings of inadequacy, remembered wounds —the freight of our adult memories of childhood. He wants and needs to be seen as a totally new human creature who will have every opportunity to see his life in his own way and who will mold himself and his experience originally and uniquely.

It is one of the most difficult tasks of parenthood—but perhaps the most rewarding—when a parent can give the supreme gift of allowing his child to be himself, to experiment with his likenesses and differences from his parents and everyone else, unimpeded in his search for his own identity by the identity problems of anyone else.

*Guilty Parents and How They Grow*  It almost never fails —each time a new mother comes into my office at the nursery school she starts the conference off by saying, "I suppose now you'll tell me all the things I'm doing wrong." What a brainwashed lot we parents are. It wasn't always thus.

A few years ago I was meeting with a group of mothers in a discussion series that took place in the home of one of the

21

group members. During one session, her mother, who was visiting, listened in on the discussion. Grandma was obviously fascinated and horrified as she sat listening to the worries and anxieties of the younger generation of mothers. She kept shaking her head in wonder and sympathy, especially during a discussion of how a mother could get her housework done, take the children out to play, and also have some time left to rest herself. After the meeting she came up to me and said that she'd enjoyed the meeting but she couldn't understand why young mothers worried so much. "You all act like you need a college education to raise children. How do you think we did it? People have been raising children for thousands of years without worrying every minute." Then she said she would give me an example of how she used to relax when she got tired as a young mother. She had eight children and she lived in a tenement on the Lower East Side. On the first balmy spring day she would line her children up, two by two, and march them several miles to Central Park. There she would find a sunny hill, and she would lie down on the grass, instructing her eight children to sit in a circle around her. She would tell the children that this was a special park for mothers to rest in but that there were kidnappers who would steal mothers. She said they must sit and guard her while she took a nap. Then, shrugging her shoulders, to show me how simple life could be if you just had good sense, she added, "They got the air and I got my rest."

I have never forgotten that charming lady or her advice because it was such a perfect example of the difference in our generations. Can you imagine how guilty a parent would feel about doing something like that today? The trauma it might cause a little psyche to hear about mother-kidnappers! Why, we would assume that our children would be scarred for life!

A French mother, after asking about the nature of my work, said very sadly that there was very little child psychology in France. "All we can do," she said apologetically, "is raise our children by the heart." I have never been able to forget that conversation because I found myself feeling that I was more to be pitied than she. It is time we learned to combine our useful new information with a little careful listening to the heart.

*Consistency*   It is hard these days to find parents who are sure about anything having to do with raising children; cruel experts have been undermining their self-confidence for almost half a century now! However there is one subject about which most parents seem positively smug, and that is that it is very important to be consistent.

I guess it is the nature of my calling to find it unbearable to leave even one area of self-assurance intact, for I am about to try to explode that notion. To further confound the issue, parental steadfastness in favor of consistency was at least in part created by experts who encouraged this line of thinking, so I am doubly the devil's advocate in taking a negative position.

What we have said, fairly consistently, is that children are eager for us to follow through on what we say; that consistent discipline is necessary and reassuring. This is true to some degree; every human being needs some guidelines, and the younger and more inexperienced you are the more this tends to be true. It is surely helpful to children to gain a general sense of what parents stand for—what they will or will not tolerate. But this should not mean that we see our roles as parents as inflexible and unchanging. This is an unreasonable and unrealistic view of the human condition.

Consistent consistency is impossible. We are creatures of changing moods—and this cannot be kept a secret from our children. There are days when you can get away with almost anything—mother will giggle and tolerate the most unbelievable shenanigans. And there are other days if you sneeze in the wrong direction hellfire and brimstone may descend

23

on your head. There are such things as cyclic moods, fatigue and depression, which can turn the most forgiving, tolerant, loving Mama into a cat on a hot tin roof.

Not only are human beings inconsistent within themselves, but the notion that any set of parents can effect a consistent partnership in dealing with their children is another silly myth. Each of us brings with us from our life experiences entirely different hang-ups. There are mothers who don't mind bad manners at the table but who foam at the mouth if pajamas are left lying on the floor. There are fathers who get ulcers if Junior doesn't fold his napkin properly but who aren't the least disconcerted if his room appears to have been ravaged in the direct path of a cyclone. There are mothers who rage when a child says, "Damn," and fathers who can tolerate far more colorful language than that. Some fathers see nothing wrong in letting the children watch the Late Show, once in awhile, while some mothers feel they have lost control over family life completely if the children are 15 minutes behind their bedtime schedule. We were born different, we grew differently, we have different peculiarities; that is part of being human and we and our children are stuck with it.

We teach our children much more about being human through our inconsistencies than our consistencies. We teach a necessary lesson in flexibility, in being able to accept a rich variety of relationships. Parental foibles prepare you for that teacher who lets you kid around some of the time, and who can be completely unreasonable one or two days a month; it prepares you for handling one Grandma one way, and another Grandma just the opposite way. You aren't surprised by the fact that you yourself feel shy and quiet sometimes and rough and ready other times, or that you can hate someone today and adore them tomorrow. Life is full of such surprises.

24

# BIBLIOGRAPHY

*Behavioral Individuality In Early Childhood* by Thomas, Birch and Chess. New York University Press, 1963.

*Disclosing Man to Himself* by Sidney Jourard, Van Nostrand, 1968.

*Don't Be Afraid of Your Child* by Hilde Bruch, M.D., Farrar, Straus and Young, 1953.

*Love and Will* by Rollo May. Norton, 1969.

*On Becoming a Person* by Carl Rogers. Houghton Mifflin, 1970.

*Personal Growth* by Clark Moustakas, Howard Doyle, 1969.

*The Inner World of Choice* by Frances Wickes. Harpers, 1963.

*The Quest for Identity* by Allen Wheelis, M.D. W.W. Norton, 1958.

*Towards a Psychology of Being* by Abraham Maslow. Van Nostrand, 1962.

*Transparent Self* by Sidney Jourard. Van Nostrand, 1964.

*Your Child Is a Person* by Thomas, Birch and Chess. Simon and Schuster, or Paralax Paperback, 1965.

This may seem like a strange list of books for parents, since many of them do not deal directly with parent-child relations. It seems to me that the best education for parenthood occurs when parents try to search out their own fundamental values —their philosophy of life—a point of view about the human experience, and these are books that have helped me greatly in my own quest for understanding.

# Chapter II

## LISTENING FOR THE FLOWERS
### The Pre-School Years

* During the pre-school years, the crucial aspects of growth are not as easily influenced by external forces as is true later on—children are then more products of their homes than of society. Usually parental concerns center on the following areas.

1. Parents feel helpless in the face of the young child's fears. How could such a happy baby become so filled with apprehension? There doesn't seem to be any way in which to give reassurance—and adults begin to feel angry because of a sense of impotence. You stand there, it's three o'clock in the morning and there is Maria screaming in terror because the lamppost outside the window makes a shadow on her wall that looks like a tiger. You turn on the lights, you feel the wall, you offer to leave the lights on, you explain that tigers are all securely locked up—but she goes on yelling, and because you are so helpless you feel as though you could strangle her!

2. Parents are panic-stricken that behavior won't change. They expect to be awakened every night forever, they are afraid that their child will always wet his bed, cling to them when other people are around, eat like a hummingbird.

* From *How to Survive Parenthood*. Pages 26–31, line 18.

3. Parents find themselves becoming perplexed and uncertain when their children begin to really rebel. We feel we are losing control, that we aren't respected. We find ourselves overreacting and we don't know why. It is hard to let go, our children are still so helpless that accepting the evidence at hand that they are becoming ready for some opportunities for independence makes us confused and uncertain. Our children's rebellion and defiance reawaken old and forgotten conflicts in our own childhood, when we too behaved in unacceptable ways, were punished and had to learn to control our impulses.

*The Magic of Words*   There are definite tendencies during the period of growth from about two to five years that seem to me to form the basis for our concerns. Language—its meaning, its use as a tool of communication—is one of the crucial growth areas; the other is an emerging sense of self, and an awareness of what it means to be a human being.

What do they do when they discover anger, jealousy, rage —the unlovely or socially unacceptable parts of being human? Let's look back for a minute at the time before language, or thinking-in-words, began. When a baby or a toddler feels uncomfortable or frustrated, it is just a generalized feeling all over his body. His face may turn red, he may howl, his body gets rigid, he may wave his arms and legs. If he is uncomfortable, if something hurts, or if he is angry because he has been left alone, all we can observe is a kind of generalized physiological reaction all over him—something for which he hasn't any words and no conscious thought. As he gets older he learns words—and one part of his developing vocabulary has to do with feelings. Now such things as love and kindness and sharing and friendliness take on form and shape. He can think in words: "I love Mommy —she gave me chocolate pudding," or, "I was a friendly boy —I shared my truck with my little brother." Children learn attitudes along with language and they figure out that certain

27

kinds of thoughts and the actions associated with them are acceptable, appreciated and desired by adults, and others are not. I suppose that if there is a culture somewhere in the world where it is considered evil to love, children at the language-learning stage of development would develop guilt feelings about being affectionate and nice! In our society, it is anger and hate, aggression and hostility, that are considered naughty or bad and have to be overcome. But they are *felt,* and now they are thoughts-in-language.

When language first develops it is quite primitive. Young children think magically. We never completely lose this quality even as adults—there is still a kind of instinctual, primitive feeling that words or thoughts can make things happen. If we talk about some good fortune we knock on wood lest some evil destroy our luck because we have to put it into words. The other day I was talking to a friend on the phone and she said that her husband might be getting a much better job. When I asked her for more details, she said, "I don't dare talk about it—wait until it's more definite." This is a holdover from childhood, when all language was so new that it seemed to have infinite and magical powers.

We think, very often, that because a young child's language is limited, we can say a great many things in front of him because "he's too young to understand." The truth of the matter is that he is too young to look at our words with the sophistication we bring to language, but he understands something. Frequently we underestimate the two- to three-year-old's reactions to a death in the family, the arrival of a new baby or any other major family crisis. He doesn't *seem* to notice or react. Several years later we may discover confusions and misconceptions that have completely distorted his view about what took place; his language was too primitive and his perceptions often strange and magical.

The language-learning child faces one of the greatest tests he will ever have to encounter—a crisis that has been written about by poets and philosophers and which figures as a cen-

28

tral theme in all religions: once you discover that being human you are imperfect and that you have angry thoughts and feelings—you really don't love everybody all the time; in fact, there are moments when you could gladly kill—what in the world can you do with this shocking information? Well, for one thing, guilt becomes part of the human experience. Whether this will be the beginning of constructive self-control or of destructive self-hatred depends on what we do to help a child through this deep personal crisis. He'll go through it no matter what—and he will hurt and he will suffer—but if we know what's going on we can help him solve his problems to some extent, so that he will be able to move on to new challenges without the deep paralysis or distortion that can stunt his emotional growth.

Some children, in becoming aware that they are partly "devil" as well as partly "angel," find a scapegoat; *they* are good—it is someone else who is bad. This is the age for the emergence of an imaginary playmate who can serve as the "shadow side" of oneself. Some children will say, "Yesterday I was the bad Billy, today I'm the good Billy." Each part is still distinct and separate even within oneself. A child comes to nursery school a pretty, dainty little lady. She kisses the teacher and then, sliding off her lap, makes an absolutely terrifying, catlike face and says, "Now I am a terrible lion. I will scratch your eyes out, and I will take my claws and then I will kill you!" Some awfully sweet and docile children are almost never themselves—they are constantly playing at being a galloping horse, a mean biting cat, a naughty little dog, a jumping rabbit who bumps into everything and knocks things over. Goodness is expressed as oneself, badness has to be externalized and disassociated from oneself because it is just too painful. Why is it painful? Because if you think bad thoughts terrible things can happen, things you really don't want to come about, but your thoughts can make them happen. Think only good thoughts and you'll be safe—the bad thoughts belong to that tiger or horse, not to you.

One night when we were trying to comfort our daughter after she had a nightmare, and talk about the dark in realistic terms, she finally said, "But I'm afraid of *my* dark," and of course this is the crux of the matter. It is at this stage of life that each of us had to face our "own dark"—the dark side of man's nature—the primitive fantasies and wishes, the uncivilized part, the part that remains the animal aspect of us. It is perceptive of our children to choose so often at this age to be afraid of animals, since in reality it is the animal in them that is so frightening.

*Mastering Fear*   There are many ways in which understanding this struggle can make life easier for parents. First of all, we can be quite sensible about it by not being afraid, as I was, that because a child is going through a period of fears and nightmares this will go on forever. It is the logical growth work for his age, and it will *not* go on forever. Secondly, we can ease the symptoms somewhat by speaking about the problem not around it. Instead of saying, "There's nothing to be scared of," we can ask, "Tell me what the thunder makes you think of," or, "What makes that kitty so scary?" and we can help our children say out loud what the qualities are that they are having such difficulty internalizing and accepting as part of themselves. I don't believe that we should ever walk around with couches on our backs and become our children's psychiatrists, nor should we ever, at any stage of growth, make our children feel that they have no privacy and that we should examine all of their thoughts. Everybody needs the right to be free in his innermost thoughts, the right to the dignity of privacy, but we can speak generally.

The magic power of words—and the thoughts they bring —this is the central issue. It can lead to paralyzing fears if unrelieved. When an especially imaginative and intensely alive child goes through this growth experience, it can block growth and learning if we don't do anything about it. One little girl went through two and a half years of never being herself when she was naughty—she would become a cat or a crocodile—and so realistically that she scared her nursery teachers! She was exceptionally bright but this absorption cut down on the amount of energy she could use for play and growth; although she could paint and do marvelous improvizations her energies were sapped by her central concern, and although she did get over it and resolved her conflict eventually so that at least she stopped being an animal, some of her talent and vitality had been wasted and even her resolution was not as good as some other children's. The reason for this was in part that try as she did, her mother simply could not accept the imperfect, the shadow part of herself, so neither could her child. The mother was a sweet, soft-spoken, sensitive person, raised by her parents to repress and push away any aggressive or angry feelings and she could not forgive herself if she lost her temper, nor could she tolerate jealousy between her children or anger expressed toward herself.

We help children most through this phase of growth when we ourselves can be tolerant of the human condition, when we have made peace with the idea that we are each many things. We strive to be civilized and social, but we also accept and try to love that part of ourselves which refuses to be tamed or intimidated by civilization; that part which can take the form of drive, vitality, creativity, imagination, and which comes with the package deal, including the primitive instinct to fight for one's individuality, to resist interference, to refuse the acceptance of compromises. When we learn to balance and accept the social and the instinctual our children also learn to live with both sides—and the best thing about this is that then our resources can be freed: we aren't using up a lot of psychic energy in keeping the dark deep secret that we are not perfect or lovable and sweet. Knowledge of our deepest and darkest parts makes it possible for us to bring them under control and to help us become the masters of our fate.

These are the years for a beginning sense of "me"—self-discovery, self-awareness—when it becomes important to do what we can to help a child get a good image of himself, an image that will help him feel he is lovable, and capable of mastering life's challenges and problems.

We know that the reason for immature behavior is because the child *is* immature, and really, we do know he'll outgrow it. But the young child doesn't know anything of the kind—his time sense is too limited, he can't imagine a time beyond tomorrow—so how can he be optimistic about getting over being immature? A cartoon showed a little boy trying to fight off being put into the dentist's chair, and saying, "You're always telling me I'm too young for this and too young for that—now all of a sudden I'm a big boy!"

Most of the things that our children do which we wish they wouldn't and which we admonish them to stop doing are normal for their age and are perfectly appropriate ways of coping with life. Crying when you're scared, for instance. This is nature's own way to help a child express fear and release the accompanying tension. When we let a child know we respect this natural reaction we release his energies to try and control it to some extent. When we make him feel ashamed and inadequate we increase the tension and force him to struggle so hard for self-control, on such a high level, that fatigue makes it twice as hard for him to cope successfully.

* *Death and Young Children*   I was standing in line at a neighborhood bank behind a young mother and her four-year-old son. It was a long line and he was impatient and jumpy. Suddenly a lovely little old lady appeared carrying two heavy shopping bags and the little boy almost jumped out of his skin with joy as he pounced on his Grandma. Her enthusiasm matched his and she offered to take him home for lunch where he could wait for his mother. In his glee, he

* From *Natural Parenthood*. Pages 32–41, line 5.

jumped up and down and knocked one of the bags out of his grandmother's hand, and as his mother began to scold him for being too wild the little old lady suddenly crumpled to the floor of the bank—and died. Of course none of us knew that immediately. The lines of people moved back, someone brought a pillow for her head, somebody else went to call the police, a bank teller ran up the block to see if a doctor was available.

I stood and watched this moving drama of life and death for some time. A doctor finally appeared and told the young woman her mother was dead. The daughter explained, "She's had a heart condition for seven years, and we've begged her not to go shopping and carry those heavy bags, but she wouldn't give in." It was clear that Grandma was in her late seventies, that she had lived her life the way she wanted to, refusing to be an invalid, and that she had died with style—still living independently, still much loved, still young in spirit. Her death seemed to me, as an adult, quite comprehensible, inevitable.

Shaken and deeply moved, it was not until I began to walk out of the bank that I thought about the little boy. Then I remembered his look of unbelieving shock—and I remembered with piercing anguish that he had sat on the floor next to his grandmother patting her arm and saying "I didn't mean to hurt you." I wanted to run back and tell his mother to be sure and explain that he hadn't killed his grandma with his loving exuberance—that she was a sick old lady and that if she'd had the choice this was undoubtedly the way she would have preferred to die—in loving encounter with her grandchild.

All of us ignored the little boy until his grandmother was taken away and he and his mother began to leave the bank, she weeping and certainly too distracted to think about her son, he wide-eyed with terror. A woman leaned toward the young mother, patted her on the shoulder as she walked by, and said, "At least he's too young to understand."

That is really the heart of the matter. Children are really *never* too young after the age of two or three to understand *something* about death. And what they usually "understand" is a complete misinterpretation of the true events. Young children tend to make self-references about almost every experience when they are little. Jean Piaget, the Swiss educator and psychologist, reported from his observations of children that until the age of nine or ten the way children think naturally involves them in every dramatic experience. If parents divorce the child thinks "It's my fault. If I wasn't so naughty, they would still love each other." If a grandparent dies, the child's irrational fantasy is, "I guess I killed Grandpa because I made noise in the hall when he was sick." If Daddy has to go away on a business trip, Junior thinks, "I'm not lovable enough to keep him here," while frequently, adopted youngsters, no matter what they have been told to the contrary, believe there must have been something wrong with them or their natural parents could not have given them up.

Whenever and where ever young children experience death they need our help in interpreting its meaning, in clarifying the fact that they are not responsible. And then they have every right to share in our grief—to cry, to feel deeply sad, to need comforting. When we say we want to protect our children from pain we really leave them alone with wild fantasies, unshed tears, and great loneliness. We don't mean to but that's what protection often seems to mean. Children and adults can only surmount grief when they understand the meaning of death and when they share their anguish and seek comfort and strength from each other.

*Spanking*  My experience has been that if you ask a group of young parents what is the subject that concerns them, very high on the list will be the matter of spanking.

I cannot see any point in discussing whether or not we *ought* to spank our children; it is an irrelevant question. Being human, it seems to me we have to assume that almost every parent who ever lived, hit his kid some time or other.

A more legitimate question: Is spanking a helpful, constructive form of discipline? No, it is not. Unequivocally! It may relieve our anger and clear the air when the atmosphere has become pretty tense and wound up, but it does not teach any constructive lessons about human relations, and, after all, that's what discipline is all about: the ways in which we try to teach our children to live in a civilized fashion with themselves and others.

The classic example of the negative teaching involved in spanking was a scene I remember well from the time when my daughter was about three and we were sitting in a park playground. A little boy of about five came over, took a swat at her, and ran off with her pail and shovel. In the midst of trying to comfort my child, wounded in soul as well as in body, I saw Mama descending upon the little boy like a wrathful God, slapping hard and howling, "*This* will teach you to hit someone smaller than you!" It occurred to me that logic was sorely missing in that all-too-familiar scene between parent and child. There seems to be a natural tendency among us parents to teach by negative example. It hardly seems likely that Junior is going to learn very much about not hitting if that is the technique he experiences himself as a parental solution to all problems.

Even when we think we are being most rational about spanking, we are still not teaching any terribly valuable lessons. We say, for example, "I have to give you a spanking in order to make you remember how dangerous it is to run across the road." The lesson there is: "Here I am, a grownup—a college graduate, even—and the only resource I have at my disposal to teach you the dangers of traffic is physical violence!" What a discouraging picture of human potential!

I believe there is only one appropriate use of spanking—and that is when one is so frightened or so angry or so impatient that one spanks without trying to rationalize or justify it at all; it just happens because you can't help it. You and

35

your child know that it is resorting to the lowest possible level of human interaction and that you don't approve of it but that sometimes things just get to be too much. If, after such an episode, you are so awash with guilt that you cannot even talk to your child about it he learns that one should feel very guilty about being human and therefore imperfect. If, out of guilt, you try to find a justification, such as "I had to do that to make you understand," you are still in trouble because you did *not* do it with premeditation, you are just plain lying to salve your own conscience. If, on the other hand, you feel a normal and civilized amount of guilt for a fall from grace and can apologize quite honestly and straightforwardly, both you and your child can pick up the pieces and move on to some better way of communicating with each other.

Parents sometimes underestimate the importance of being able to say "I'm sorry" to a child. It is one of the best lessons in discipline for its message is simply this: "People sometimes lose control. If they are decent, sensible, grown-up people, they try hard to be reasonable but sometimes they lose control, because living with kids can be pretty trying. But the great thing about human beings is that they can always strive to improve."

The job of being a grown-up parent is of course to try to increase our sensitivity, our responsibility, so that we resort to primitive behavior as infrequently as possible—and that we don't try to justify brutal or harshly punitive actions as being worthy of the label "sound discipline." At the same time it is not necessary to get out the sackcloth and ashes or to give ourselves thirty lashes whenever we spank. Children are great forgivers; they know when we are scared or when we have reached the end of our endurance, and they do not see our momentary loss of control as a terrible threat to their well-being. Quite the contrary; when you are little and weak and very much in the grip of impulses you often cannot control, it is very comforting to discover that those giants of strength, your parents, have their imperfections, too.

Spanking has no great lessons to teach about wisdom and self-control, but until some sort of mutant—a new species of superior men—arrives on this planet we are stuck with it.

*On Being Fair*   One of the most difficult challenges in being a parent is that children frequently do not say what they really mean. We find ourselves responding to their *words,* rather than to the background music. And then when we begin to realize that our responses have been meaningless or futile we despair of being good enough detectives to figure out what is really going on.

A good case in point is what happens when our children tell us that we are not being fair: Johnny got a bigger piece of cake than Suzy, an older child complains that a younger one stays up just as late as he does, Karen is mad because Jeff was allowed to buy a comic book on a shopping trip but no one brought her one. Because it is of course impossible to love any two human beings in exactly the same way we become frightened by the challenge "You're not being fair." We wonder if we *are* showing partiality—we try to mend our ways. It seems to me that we would be more sure of our ground if we could figure out what that indictment of unfairness really means. Let's take a closer look at some real-life situations:

A mother recently reported that she had solved the bedtime problem at her house. Her three-year-old felt she was being treated unfairly when she had to go to bed before her two older brothers, so mother had talked the boys into pretending they were going to sleep at the same time. Once she was asleep the boys were allowed to get up and play a little longer. A father said that he was on his way home from work one night and suddenly had an impulse to get his daughter a gift. She had been quite sick and had behaved very well

37

and he wanted to let her know he felt proud of her. He started to buy her a toy, then began to wonder if the two younger children would be jealous and think he was unfair, so he bought presents for them, too. When he walked into his daughter's room and gave her the gift, her face lighted up— she got the message—and then, when her father went on to give presents to the other children, her pleasure ended as quickly. He knew that something had gone wrong in his wish not to show favoritism.

Children encourage our confusion about what is fair. They sense very quickly that we are uncertain, sensitive, inclined to be on the defensive. How ought we to respond? It seems to me very probable that the taunt "You're being unfair" is really a challenge—a question: "Am I special? Do you see me as a separate person?" This is more important to all human beings than absolute equality. The little girl mentioned earlier isn't going to be satisfied by her mother's solution to the problem of bedtime for very long, and neither are her brothers. The present brought to the sick child had no special meaning because all three children got something at that moment.

It is actually enormously reassuring to a child when a parent agrees with his complaint of unfairness completely and says, "Yes, you are absolutely right—I don't treat you and Jack the same way, and I don't give you the same things, because you are two completely different people, and what may be important and good for one may not be for the other." If children find us constantly trying to be fair in some unrealistic way they are likely to continue to complain of unfairness, even if we eventually get a gram scale and measure everything out carefully! They will continue this complaint because the answer has been unsatisfactory. Frantic attempts at equalizing tell a child that his parents don't see him as a separate person—and that they probably *do* have a favorite or why would they go to such lengths to disprove it?

38

Unfairness goes with individuality. What may be right for one youngster may be wrong for another. Intense caring, individual concern, are far more meaningful than equality. What is *really* fair is when children feel they are being seen separately—when they observe that our sense of justice is based on individual needs and not on comparisons. The outraged cry "You're being unfair!" is a trap. Let's not fall into it. There will be far less weighing of justice in our households when we respond "You're darned right!"

*"Black is Beautiful" Isn't Enough*  Ever since the words, "Black is Beautiful" were first chanted, I have been worrying about whether or not this phrase was really going to be helpful to black children. I understand its necessity and I am in complete sympathy with its social and political implications, but the psychologist in me remains restless! What bothers me most of all is that I want black Americans to remember that if pride in one's group identity were enough there ought not to be so many white people who grow up hating themselves so bitterly!

I was reminded of this by an incident that I witnessed during the summer. My husband and I were sunbathing beside a motel pool that had one of those slides that shoot right into the water. It was quite high and I heard an adult comment that even she found it scary at the top. A little girl of about five was playing very happily and privately at the shallow end of the pool until her parents came into the water. For the next twenty minutes—until I was just too horrified and unhappy to stay any longer and went inside—we watched a scene that is typical of what all parents do at one time or another to their children, white or black, that makes it very difficult for a child to grow up with a good image of himself. Apparently there had been some previous discussion about Linda's going on the slide the day before and she had cried. The campaign now started anew with threats and promises, wheedling, and such charming and helpful

39

judgments as; "You're a big baby—what's the matter with you—you're such a scaredy cat." There was an assumption that filled the air around that little girl, that something was wrong with *her*.

It is a small incident—not very exciting or dramatic. And yet it is repeated ten thousand times a day (in the homes of America) and whether the children are white or black it is the kind of act that produces a hatred of the child within oneself that is the source of more adult agony than anything else.

It is impossible to become a fulfilled, warmly loving, creatively growing adult if within oneself there is this unloved, awful child—this view one got of oneself through the eyes of parents who undoubtedly meant well but did not realize how powerful and omnipotent they seemed to a small child.

It is a natural human reaction to feel awfully imperfect as a child and to distort what appear to be the failures of childhood into a whole condemnation of oneself. That little girl being pushed to go down the slide was white—but if her parents go on pushing—about reading, or skating, or not being shy or learning to dance with boys—it won't matter one bit that she's white—she will *still* grow up hating herself, unable to become most deeply and truly herself.

I would hope, therefore, that black parents will of course try to impart a sense of racial and historical pride as one dimension of helping their children grow to full adulthood—but that they would understand this is only the beginning. The *real* glory for *any* human being is to feel, "To be *me* is beautiful!" That black parents would understand what white parents are still struggling with, that pride comes down finally to a sense of self, the right to be what one is—and that any kind of pushing, any kind of driving, ambitious, agressive demands that growth come when we want it, in the ways we want it, will only twist and distort it. If what follows "Black is beautiful" is, "And Baby, you're going to conquer the world!" the young, shy, growing thing inside the

40

child shrivels. If instead one says, "Black is beautiful—and you are beautiful because you are a special person—wonderful just being yourself"—Ah then there will be the kind of strength and resourcefulness and inner pride we are really seeking.

\* *Nursery School*   Nursery education is "in" at long last. For those of us who have felt that going to nursery school could be a profoundly meaningful experience for most young children, this should be a time of great exultation and triumph. It is not. The current vogue to support pre-school education has very little to do with the values which motivated the pioneers in nursery-school education; who saw it as an opportunity to help young children explore their own three-to-five world, to encourage creativity and self-understanding, and to provide opportunities for learning to live well with other people.

When any young child expresses a genuine interest and readiness for a new experience it would of course be ridiculous to hold him back, whether this be learning to write his name, count to 100, or swim. The point is that, quite aside from this issue, *where are we going in such a hurry?* A child who develops such skills at three or four will not necessarily be any more skilled at eight than children who learn such skills at seven. But whether or not he *does* perform at a higher level, of what consequence is this in the life of a human being whom we have every reason to believe will still be writing, counting, and swimming at eighty?

The brains of three- and four-year-olds have become a "national asset"—to be exploited, to be pushed into more rapid growth, to solve all the problems of later school failures. We act as if we had found a relatively simple answer to one of the most complicated and terrifying problems facing education today. In an urban and industrial society faced with impossible problems of population explosion, in-

\* From *The Conspiracy Against Childhood*. Pages 41–50, line 14.

adequate teachers and schools, with educational programs that are unequal to the tasks involved in meeting the problems of rapid and complex social change, we have decided that the primary solution to our problems is to start formal education at an earlier age. Despite the fact that the increase in school failures is not only a problem of the "culturally deprived" child but is also occurring more frequently among his more privileged middle-class schoolmates, reflecting school systems in which classes are too large, in which educational services are drowning in a sea of administrative functions and which, with the best will in the world, no teacher however dedicated and gifted can possibly meet the varied and complex needs of each child, we seem bent on making our three- to-five-year olds solve the problem of the glaring inadequacies of our school systems.

Walk with me into a nursery-school classroom; let us see what a group of three-to-four-year-olds are up to. In the doll corner Robbie is curled up in the doll crib; he is sucking his thumb and talking baby talk. Patty is making believe she is his mother, and she says, "Now just stop making such a fuss—I'm fixing your bottle as fast as I can. If you start to cry I am going to be very mad at you!" Dennis, who said he wanted to be the daddy, seems to have changed his mind. He is crawling around on all fours and as he reaches the side of the crib he says, "Don't worry, baby, I am a fierce and terrible lion, but I won't hurt you."

At a table nearby, three or four children are drawing pictures of guitars, drums, bugles, tambourines and bells. Their drawings are crude, and by the time their pictures have been colored in, cut out and pasted on a large board, they may look more like abstract than representational artwork; but they are making a poster which will announce to their classmates that tomorrow they are going to have a "concert." For several weeks they been looking at, touching, playing with an assortment of instruments brought in by their teacher and shown to all the children. These are the children who were intrigued, who wanted to play with them, and they are very clear about which ones you bang and which ones you blow and which ones you "go pling-pling." While they are absorbed in their advertisement campaign they are having a noisy conversation. Penny says, "At my house I have fifty hundred toys!" Jennifer replies disapprovingly, "You do not —you're making that up." Peter says, "You stop yelling or I'm gonna hit you both"—then, looking up surreptitiously to see if any teacher has heard him, he smiles sheepishly and says, "I'll let you come to *my* house. I got new skates. My Daddy doesn't live in my house anymore but he says he's gonna take me skating in the park."

Two boys are lying on the floor gazing at the ceiling. Nearby is a tower of blocks that they have just built. It is a "rocket," and they are pretending that they are spacemen, about to take off. Three or four little girls are washing doll clothes in the bathroom, laughing hysterically because "soap-suds look like pee-pee."

Let us "cut the scene" right there. On the face of it are these children "learning" anything? Before we decide that they are wasting their time in idle fancy and ought to be learning the alphabet, let us hear what the teacher can tell us about them. Robbie, the current crib occupant, is a shy, lonely little boy who for the first four weeks of nursery school stayed almost entirely on the sidelines. When invited to enter into an activity with the other children he would smile but move quickly away. Almost four, he is the oldest of three children; his days for being the baby in the family must surely have been severely limited. Today, all of a sudden, Patty, a big, somewhat bossy youngster, said, "Robbie, I want you to play house and be the baby." Maybe Robbie had done enough watching to be ready to play; maybe the chance to play baby was just too tempting. At any rate there he is getting a chance through the marvel of make-believe to enjoy the gratification of being a baby and finding him-self at long last a member of the group. Patty's mother has told the teacher that she often loses her temper; she is ashamed that she has so little patience with a young child, and she is afraid that Patty feels she pushes her too hard. Patty plays the same kind of mother; perhaps this is one of the ways in which she comes to understand and accept her mother's human fallibility. By playing a mother's role she almost experiences a mother's feelings and can, perhaps, come closer to understanding herself and her mother. Dennis is a wild one! His parents are both European and believe in being very strict; none of this soft-headed American nonsense from them! When Dennis is naughty he gets the strap; if he talks back he goes to bed without any supper. When Dennis arrived at nursery school he was a very angry young man. During his first week of school, drunk with new freedom, he bit two children and kicked seven or eight others, and whenever the group went outdoors he ran away from the teacher and tried to open the gate out into the street. Slowly his behavior has been changing; his teacher has talked to him calmly and affectionately about how all children feel angry sometimes, and it is all right in school to talk about it but she cannot let him hurt other people any more than she can let other people hurt him. Dennis has made clay figures of "big people" and socked and punched the clay into abject submission. He has tried, over and over again, to see what the teachers will do to him if he disobeys them, and each time that he has had to be separated from the group "until you feel steady again," he has seemed more friendly and cheerful about this. He seems now to believe it when the teacher says, "When you're little you sometimes need a grown-up to help you be steady." Nothing has absorbed him more than playing with toy tigers and lions and he has spent hours building cages for them with blocks, "locking them up *tight* so they can't get out." His teacher has agreed with him and said, "Yes, wild things mustn't be allowed to hurt people." A few times she has added, "Sometimes angry feelings are like wild animals," and Dennis has looked at her thoughtfully and then grinned. For the past day or two he has rushed into the classroom, given his teacher a bear hug and exclaimed, "You're my friend!" Now he is the lion-daddy but he tells shy Robbie that despite his wild feelings he won't hurt him.

The music lovers have been drawing, cutting and pasting, and practicing all the small-muscle controls that they are beginning to be able to master; they have worked in unison on a common interest; they have learned about wind, string and percussion instruments. They are even practicing the art of social conversation. Penny covers her uncertainties about herself by boasting; Jennifer knows this may be "real" to Penny, but she sternly makes it clear it isn't *really* real"— as both children go on experimenting with fantasy and reality in order to eventually master the differences. And, for the first time since the event six months before, Peter has been able to say out loud to somebody else, "My Daddy is gone." Although his teachers have known of the divorce Peter has been telling them at least once a day about how his Daddy is going to come home tonight and play with him. His teacher has said, "Peter, I know how much you want that to happen," and now she exults as she hears that Peter has faced up to the holocaust in his young and vulnerable life

Our two spacemen have never played together before. They are both big, blustery, restless children. At first they seemed overly aggressive and excitable; now it seems that perhaps they were bored until they found each other. They are bright, alert, curious, and now that they have discovered each other the teachers know there will hundreds of questions, books needed to look up information they want, all kinds of special adventures in learning that they can share and that they alone are ready for. They really love each other! How infinitely precious it is to each of them to have found such a friend.

The giggling laundresses were infants just a year ago; they could suck on their fingers, they could wet their pants—they may even, if we may assume they are normal, have had one heck of a good time smearing their feces on the side of the crib in some delightful undiscovered moment. It is still fun to feel things that are wet and squashy—and it is even more fun, when among friends, to talk about things that some grown-ups say are naughty. Their teacher has explained, "When you are alone you may talk about bathroom things, but when you are with grown-ups some of them may feel unfriendly if you talk that way." This kind of social distinction is just beginning to penetrate.

If these children are "wasting the nation's time," we are in more trouble than we know. Each in his own way, in *play*, is finding his own answers to some weighty and vital problems; in play that is fun and absorbing and challenging each one is learning. It is easy to recognize how a child may enhance his physical growth as he learns to jump, run, climb, balance, swing, push, pull, or ride a bicycle. It ought to be equally clear to perceptive and sensitive adults that children come to a deeper understanding of themselves and others when they pretend to be storekeepers, policemen, wild animals, farmers, doctors, or bridge builders. When a child moves into group play, when he shares or takes turns, when he recognizes another's pain or frustration, when he acts out his own conflicts, anxieties, fears and confusions, in a world of make-believe, he is doing the plain, hard, uncompromising *work* of growing up. He is challenged by his environment to create, imagine, explore, experiment, fail and succeed, and in the process he begins to learn who he is, what he can do, what it means to live and work in harmony with others. This may well represent some of the hardest work he will ever have to do—and if he can do it with joy, with instinctive, playful pleasure, isn't that a blessing!

Increasing consciousness and awareness of this world that one has fallen into makes the life tasks of three-to-five-year-olds overwhelming, in view of all these profound and complex questions they are beginning to face. And the best tool they have for beginning to find answers is play. If we sit them down at a table and say, "Be quiet and count these beads," we are robbing them of the opportunity to struggle with questions that need thinking about and studying, through the explorations of free, spontaneous, self-directed play experiences. Playing "going to the hospital" can relieve and release both real and fantasied fears about that recent tonsillectomy; pretending to be a mean tough cowboy with a gun can help a young child express aggressive feelings that must not be directed toward other people; making believe that one is a policeman can help a child internalize the controls he needs over his antisocial impulses; building a town with blocks can help him gain information and mastery of a small part of the world he observes.

Educators have known about these values in play for as long as there have been researchers in psychiatry and psychology, and the encouragement and enrichment of play have been of central concern to the large majority of educators throughout the past fifty years. I do not believe that most of the specialists who work in the field of nursery education have lost their commitment, their enthusiasm, for a child's right to his play anymore than I have; but they seem to have become less vocal about it in the past few years. I think that all of us have been too easily intimidated by a small but very vocal minority of educators and psychologists who offer today's parents the alternatives that so many parents want most —that seem to alleviate their anxiety about a child's academic achievement. Today's parents, caught in the general hysteria about the need for a college education are open to any voice that promises a magic formula for making children learn quickly. The rest of us, too reasonable and too open-minded, I am afraid, have become passive spectators while our children are fed to the technician-lions.

If I were looking for a nursery school that would best meet the needs of my own child, these are the qualities I would look for:

1. I would want a child-oriented setting, which provides stimulation and opportunity for children to develop those skills that are appropriate to their age, needs, and interests. There would be a great deal of equipment to encourage dramatic and imaginative play. There would be creative materials, such as paints and clay, to encourage expression of feelings. There would be equipment for releasing the energy and vitality of young children, helping them to develop the large-muscle coordination they want and are ready for. It would be a place with space, with room to run and jump and move freely.

2. I would want a warm and accepting environment peopled by teachers who know a great deal about the psychological needs of young children and can help them cope with their genuine struggle to become human—to be free and to be themselves but in a context of relating to others. I would want teachers who are ready to experiment, to explore, to let the child's curiosity and spirit of adventure lead to unplanned learning and discovery, where new questions are encouraged and answers found together.

3. I would want to know if the teachers are content to be with three- and four-year-olds and see enough excitement in this—free of a terrible sense of urgency to turn these children into six- and seven-year-olds.

4. I would want a school that is open to change and to new ideas but not easily swayed by the passing fashion of the moment. The teachers must feel free to experiment with new equipment, new methods, but only in the context of retaining critical judgment and preserving a basic philosophy that is well-balanced and clearly thought out.

5. I would want to see teachers who are not impressed by surface learning—who know that young children are won-

48

derful mimics and can be taught to repeat information, but who know that this has nothing whatever to do with deeper understandings. I would want teachers who encourage a child to learn as much and as fast as he pleases, but who do not measure their own value or status by the learning they can see—teachers who are satisfied with their work only when they know that what is being learned is meaningful and is meeting all the needs of a young child, whether or not the satisfaction can be measured or seen.

6. I would choose a school where children are on the move; where the program is flexible and relaxed enough so that children can begin to make their own decisions, where being quiet or active are choosable commodities most of the time. I do not want permission for chaos; there must be regulations and rules whenever groups of people try to live together. I would want a room full of opportunities, where chatter and movement and changing interests and activities are not merely viewed as permissible but are deliberately encouraged. Reasonable rules about safety and respect for property and the rights of others should be enforced by grown-ups who do not expect young children to be capable of self-control all at once.

7. I would seek an environment in which children ask whatever questions they want and where teachers help children find their own answers; an environment in which teachers are concerned about the child who *always* needs to be playing in a group as well as the child who *never* plays with others; about the child who never lets himself go and the child who is always at the mercy of his impulses and feelings.

8. I would want a school that is concerned with encouraging spontaneity and joy in self-expression as well as with helping children learn ways to live comfortably and creatively with others, respecting his own rights and the rights of others. Teachers in such a climate want to encourage each child to be different, to be himself, to find his own inner

music, the things that will make his life significant to him; they want to help him solve whatever problems he may have that keep him from being unique and free.

Finally, I would look for a school in which teachers were not concerned with "raising I.Q.'s" but with raising a child's pleasure in the wonders of the world and the wonders within himself; where their goal is helping children to live warmly and securely with others, both with adults and other children; helping children find pleasure in developing new skills; helping each child to feel good about himself—to feel that he is a worthwhile and growing person; helping each child to understand himself and others, to gain in self-discipline and, most of all, *to like the person he is becoming.* Such a world lets each child know that he has *time to grow.*

\* *Room for Flower-Hearers*    When we can understand the life work of the pre-schooler, and when we can respect his way of growing and of gaining mastery over himself and his environment, we help him to learn his most crucial lesson, which begins at this age and goes on for the rest of his life: how to live artistically with oneself and others, how to listen to one's own inner voice and be oneself, and still live with compassion and sensitivity for others. Approval and acceptance of one's own way of growing is one way. A feeling of safety to be oneself and to learn in one's own way is another.

I read an article a number of years ago where the writer described a nursery group in which the teacher was trying to help children increase their awareness of their own senses. She held up a flower and asked the children what senses they could use in appreciating the flower. Dutifully the children said, "We can see the flower with our eyes, we can smell the flower with our noses, we can touch the flower with our hands." But then one little boy said, "And I can hear the flower." The teacher responded, "Oh no, Johnny, we can't

\* From *How to Survive Parenthood.* Pages 50–52, line 13.

hear the flower." And the observer wrote: "What kind of world would it be without those who can hear flowers—what of our poets and dreamers, who help the rest of us to hear flowers?" In our contacts with young children we can help them communicate and feel good about themselves if we leave plenty of room for flower-hearers.

Many years ago I heard a story that still moves me deeply. When the United Nations met at Lake Success on New York's Long Island, a nursery school was set up for the children of the delegates. Teachers had to be sensitive to many differences, they had to speak several languages, and they were a devoted and dedicated group. The children came from all parts of the world. One time a Chinese delegate arrived in New York. During the flight to America his wife had become very ill and when the plane landed an ambulance was waiting to rush her to the hospital. The delegate was needed at some important meetings and so he had to bring his four-year-old son to the nursery school. The child knew no English, he had just flown from his home to a totally strange and unfamiliar land, and as if that wasn't enough, in transit he had even lost the comfort of his mother's presence.

When his father brought him to school he accepted the situation without protest and simply stood quietly, weeping. He was inconsolable, he would not let anyone touch him, he would not play or eat or take a nap. He stood all day long, quietly brushing away his tears. None of the teachers could speak Chinese, and they were greatly distressed about this little boy's misery. That first night one of the teachers went to Chinatown and bought some Chinese toys. Another teacher was able to find a Chinese picture book. But the same pattern occurred the next day and the next. At the point when the teachers really felt desperate about helping this little boy a strange event took place. An American girl went over to the little boy and said something to him that sounded like gibberish or nonsense-words. The boy looked up very seriously, took her hand and went with her to the table. Still

51

holding hands, with the little girl still making sounds that no one could understand, he ate some lunch. Later the two children, still holding hands, lay down on cots pulled next to each other. Still later they sat holding hands in the sandbox. The teachers were terribly curious about what was going on and delighted at the turn of events. When it was time to go home and the Chinese boy had been called for by his father a teacher asked Anne what she had done to help Lee so much. Anne said, "Well, I thought about it a lot and I couldn't talk Chinese and he couldn't talk American so I decided to talk to him in make-believe Chinese."

That is the artistry of living, and it can begin to happen very, very early in a child's life.

## TOPICS FOR PARENT MEETINGS
## AND DISCUSSION GROUPS

Because the parent discussions on the television program *How Do Your Children Grow?* were open and unstructured many topics came up at each session, making it almost impossible to provide specific subject matter areas for each program. In order to get a real sense of the ways in which individual topics were explored it is really necessary to watch the series of discussions as they unfolded, and as the threads of ideas and topics were woven together.

However, in order to provide some assistance to those who may want to use individual programs as a springboard for small group discussions, in PTA's and other community groups, we have tried to find a central theme which emerged each time. The programs dealing with the pre-school years were therefore given the following titles:

1. *"That* will teach you not to hit someone smaller than you!" (How do we discipline? For what purposes? Is spanking an effective means of educating for good human relations? What are our goals in disciplining young children?)

2. "Maybe if we didn't tell brothers and sisters they were related . . ."

    (Competition and rivalry, sibling relations)

3. "No fair being fair."

    (Is there such a thing as equality in meeting the needs of each child? Does it help to make "justice" a goal in human relationships? What does it mean to be fair to each child?)

4. "What's the turtle doing when he's supposed to be in heaven?"

    (Can a young child handle abstract ideas, such as heaven? How does he view such words? How does the pre-schooler begin to come to terms with the emerging idea of mortality? How can we best help him through this challenging and frightening experience? What methods does he find on his own?)

5. "Did Granpa die 'cause I made too much noise?"

    (The young child's misinterpretations of facts that confuse him. The developmental tendency to personalize, and to feel guilty about events that were in no way the child's responsibility. A continuing discussion of death.)

6. "I hope I don't have people-eating dreams."

    (The fantasies of young children. How do they come to terms with a growing awareness of human fallibility? How do they begin to handle feelings of hostility? The child's interpretation of his feelings of guilt and unworthiness—his preoccupation with what makes him behave in angry or hostile ways.)

7. "The *me* nobody loves."

    (What do young children need from parents, most of all? The lifetime significance of feelings of personal worth—of deep and abiding sense of being lovable.)

8. "Where have all the people who hear flowers gone?"

    (Individual differences. Respect for each child's unique ways of being and becoming most profoundly himself.)

In general, during these eight sessions, the parents of pre-schoolers discussed these major issues:

What worries parents of pre-schoolers?

1. They are concerned about the fact that their children seem to be developing new fears and phobias.
2. They see behavior that troubles them, and have the feeling it will never change.
3. They are faced for the first time by genuine rebellion.
4. They are often trying to raise their children in ways that they did not experience in their own growing-up years.
5. Parents are often hampered in dealing with the pre-school child by their lack of conscious memories of their own experiences at this age.

Parents of pre-schoolers are thinking a great deal about:

Discipline, consistency, punishments
The meaning of play
The meaning of learning
Lying
Children's fears (wild animals, thunder, the dark, etc.)
The meaning of language to the young child
Sibling relations, equality, fairness, jealousy, sharing
Children's fantasies
Death and dying
Illness and hospitalization
Running away
Realities such as separation and divorce
A child's feelings about being "good" or "bad"
Parent's rights—what bothers us, what we are most sensitive about in our children's behavior. The importance of our own lives, apart from being parents
Handling of angry feelings; difference between allowing feelings to be expressed, and actual behavior
The quality and quantity of time spent with children
What we bring of our own past into our feelings about young children
Learning to "read a child's behavior"
Awareness of constitutional differences in children
The young child's concern with social issues
Sex education

The beginning processes of separation between parent and child

## SUPPLEMENTARY RESOURCES

(For detailed information on the agencies that make films, plays, monologues, books and pamphlets available, see Chapter Five.)

Since films and plays are a familiar form of entertainment, let me just add a few words of explanation about the Monologues that are listed in Chapters Two, Three and Four:

Many years ago, when I was Director of Education of the Guidance Center in New Rochelle, New York, and doing a great deal of program planning, I began to feel that while many plays and films were quite excellent they did have some practical limitations. Many of them were quite long —more than a half hour in length, so that if they were presented at a parents' meeting they might set quite rigid limits on the amount of discussion that was possible afterwards— especially in schools where the Custodian would quite naturally like to get home at a reasonable hour! Plays involved either the expense of hiring a professional company (within a 50-mile radius of New York) or all the complications of trying to find five or six people to perform the play, and all the difficulties of arranging for adequate rehearsal time.

I suppose I would have continued to put up with these shortcomings, if, at this time, I hadn't met a young woman, Mrs. Judith Menken. She had been an actress, but now she (in the 1950s) preferred to be at home with her young children. However, she was active in the work of The Guidance Center and she asked me what I thought of the idea of her writing and performing short monologues which could be used for discussion of parent-child relationships. The first one she wrote was *Goodnight Billy,* listed in this chapter, and this

55

has been followed by many, many more, much to my delight.

The advantages of the monologues is that they provide a "live" experience with a performer, are very short, and can be read aloud if the performer prefers to do it that way. In ten minutes they provide rich material for group discussion.

Since my leaving The Guidance Center, Mrs. Menken has continued to write monologues for The Nassau County Mental Health Association, in cooperation with Mrs. Sadie Hofstein, their Mental Health Consultant. As her own children have grown, the subjects of Mrs. Menken's monologues have moved from the concerns of pre-school parents to those of teen-agers. There is further mention of the monologues in Chapter Five.

*Monologues For Pre-School Parent Groups*
    *Goodnight Billy* by Judith Menken. Sleeping problems, nightmares, fears, rivalry, understanding behavior, discipline. Nassau County Mental Health Assoc., 186 Clinton St., West Hempstead, N.Y. 10 min. 1 person. 50¢.
    *Timmy Goes To School.* Parent and child adjustment to the first school separation. All information same as above.

*Films For Pre-School Parent Groups*
    *Al in the Hospital.* 22 min. A Robert Disraeli Film, for rental info., Robert Disraeli Films, P.O. Box 343, Cooper Station, New York, N.Y. 10013. Young child has bicycle accident, is hospitalized with broken leg. For discussion of preparing children for hospitalization or any other frightening experiences.
    *Fears of Children.* 20 min. Mental Health Film Board. Rental, New York University Film Library, 29 Spring St. New York, N.Y. An older film, but a classic one. Five-year-old's normal fears and parental anxieties and reactions. Fears, overprotection, understanding behavior, ways of helping child deal with normal feelings.
    *Long Time to Grow.* Part I. 35 min. Two- and Three-Year-Olds, Vassar College Nursery School. Also an old film but an excellent picture of this developmental stage. How and what children are learning through play, needs and interests.
    Part II, 30 min. is on four- and five-year-olds.

Rental information, from New York University Film Library, address above.

*The World of Three.* 28 min. The world as seen through a three-year-old's eyes. A new film and excellent. Contemporary Films, 330 W. 42nd St., New York, N.Y. 10036. Rental, $8.00.

## Plays For Pre-School Parent Groups

*According to Size* by Nora Stirling. 25 min. Attitudes about discipline. A classic. Mental Health Materials Center, 419 Park Ave. S., New York, N.Y. 10016. $1.50, one copy, $6.00 for a performing packet of scripts. 20–30 min.

*There Was a Little Boy* by Barbara Davidson. Can really be used at any age level, since it provides an overall view of parent-child relations, but might be especially helpful to parents of young children, in thinking ahead. Written for The Play Schools Association, 120 W. 57th St., New York, N.Y. 10019. $2.00 for one copy, packet of scripts, $12.00.

## Books and Pamphlets

*Behavior: The Unspoken Language of Children* ed. by Mildred Rabinow. Child Study Assoc., 9 E. 89th St., New York, N.Y. 10028. 35¢.

*Learning to Love and Let Go* by Greta Mayer and Mary Hoover. Child Study Assoc. (see above) 75¢.

*The First Big Step* by Patricia Platt. Nat'l School Public Relations Assoc. 1201 16th St. N.W. Washington, D.C. 20036. 60¢.

*The Magic Years* by Selma Fraiberg. Scribner's, 1959.

*The Inner World of Childhood* by Frances Wickes. Appleton-Century, 1930.

*The Nursery School* by Katherine Reed, Saunders, 1960.

*The Wonderful Story of How You Were Born* by Sidonie Gruenberg. Sex and Family Life Ed. for children. New ed. Doubleday, 1970.

# Chapter III

## PASSING THE FIRE-BUILDING TESTS
### The Grade School Years

* When children arrive at school age one of our greatest fears is that now, when they are more influenced by their peers, we will lose control. And of course this is true to some extent. This is a time for a widening world of influence, inevitably, but home controls are still of the greatest significance.

As parents we feel the full impact of social disapproval from others when our children are rude, noisy, or mischievous. When they get into trouble at school a new theme enters our lives—"The Guidance Counsellor Blues." No matter how compassionate, accepting and sensible teachers, social workers and psychologists may be, parents discover themselves being measured and found wanting and where personal feelings of failure may already have occurred, one now feels that one's failures are on public display.

School-age children aren't so cute any more; they are not always lovable if we want to be honest about it. They squirm, they jiggle, they twitch, they run in packs, they are noisy and sloppy, and they never remember to do anything we ask. Worst of all, they don't think much of us anymore—we have lost our halos forever; practically *anybody* is smarter than

* From *How to Survive Parenthood*. Pages 58–62, line 29.

a parent. And then, just when we think we can't stand the feet kicking under the table one more minute, or the droopy socks, or the silly giggling that is so loud the house shakes— just then something marvelous happens. We look out a window and see a son courageously resisting group pressures to exclude the new child on the block from a game; Helen tells us that she's decided to be a veterinarian and has arranged to meet her science teacher after school to dissect a frog; Bob offers to dry the dishes on a day when you were too weary even to ask.

For all the external appearance of things, school-age children are sensitive, idealistic, proud, and eagerly curious creatures. Given a lot of room for real adventure and exploration—their own kind, not what we decide is good and then supervise for them—they can take off and fly. It is so hard for most adults to tolerate the outward behavior of school-age children that a good many wings do get clipped. There is a very real difference in today's attitudes toward mischief—no longer any room for "boys will be boys." Society will not tolerate what was once accepted and taken for granted—that childhood is a time for explosive energy and vitality, secret and impulsive and anti-adult activities.

The first rule for enjoying the fives-to-twelves is to tolerate what this age group is like, naturally and inevitably, and *not* spend hours every day in desperation and worry because these savages will never be tamed. Time and living change a great many things without our having to be in there doing battle every minute. One mother told me how she had learned to wait. When Fred, her first child, was three years old, she congratulated herself because she was doing a good job of giving him the habit of cleanliness; why, he could sit in the bathtub playing with his boats for hours and you had to drag him out. He wasn't just clean, he was "blue-white!" But when he got to be about nine his mother really was worried—where had she failed, what had happened to all her earlier training? Fred was now allergic to water. It took

59

days of imploring, hours of dire threats, to get him into the bathtub once a week, and at that, he made it quite clear she was torturing him more diabolically than if she had used the rack. What could she do to make him change? Suddenly, when he was twelve, she noticed that it was very hard for any other member of the family to get into the bathroom— Fred was doing his hair. This involved a long shower, followed by an hour or so in front of the mirror with a comb and some kind of hair goo. Fred testily asked where his clean shirt was and sometimes took two showers in one day. She started to congratulate herself—after all, her nagging had paid off, she had done a good job—and then, suddenly, she stopped kidding herself: it was that beautiful little girl who sat in front of Fred at school. "With my younger children I just relaxed, and exactly the same sort of sequence of events took place. I didn't have to do a thing!"

If we spend all of our time trying to make our children outgrow their age instead of letting time do much of the work, we can really lose touch with them and spend a good deal of time alone and angry. Another mother told me that she had been nagging her son Jeff to hang up his pajamas before he went to school and she was getting nowhere. One morning when she had a lot to do and was feeling put upon, she walked into his room and found his pajamas rolled up in a ball on the floor, all his dresser drawers open, absolute chaos inside, and the bed unmade—she decided in seething wrath that she had *had* it and that he was going to get it. All day while he was at school she muttered and growled and planned her attack for when he returned. A little after three when he galloped up the front walk she had the door open and was waiting with ammunition ready. The eager, excited look on Jeff's face disappeared as Mama yelled. He became grim and quiet; without another word he went upstairs, slammed his door, didn't emerge until dinner, seemed more angry and hurt than his mother had dreamed would be the result—she had succeeded too well. Jeff said almost nothing

60

while eating then slunk off to do his homework. A friend arrived, dashed into the house to see Jeff and shouted on the way upstairs, "Isn't it *marvelous* about Jeff being chosen from the whole school to be on that radio program?" This was the news event Jeff never got a chance to report. His mother said, "I learned something that day. I learned that if you want to be friends with a child and if you want to have the good times you need with him, you just can't waste so much time in yelling and nagging. You have to make a choice: take them as they are and get some fun out of it or turn into a shrew and hate yourself and your child almost all of the time. I could just as well have said quietly, 'Before you do anything else, Jeff, you have to clean up your room.' I didn't have to harbor all that rage and self-pity all day."

Being tolerant of what is natural doesn't mean becoming a mat that children can walk on. If you live with children you just have to expect that there will be noise and mess and excitement and a general atmosphere of disorganized living, but while we can try to tolerate some of this, it is a two-way tolerance program; children have to tolerate us, too. We have rights that must also be respected; maybe their own rooms are chaotic, but we have a right to an orderly living room; it may be noisy with lots of friendly children around, devouring every scrap in the refrigerator, on a couple of afternoons or on a Saturday or Sunday, but there are other times when the house is to be quiet and parents are to be allowed to take a nap or read a book or the newspaper in peace. We will do what we can to help our children have time for running, jumping, shouting and "messing around," but at the same time we will make it quite clear that there are some rules and laws which are to be respected.

We have to let our children know where we stand. Do we respect the tasks which are set before them during these years? Do we really know what they are working at? Someone once asked a ten-year-old what kind of work he wanted to do when he was grown-up. "I thought I was working now," he replied with dignity. There are serious, earnest and difficult tasks which our children face during the elementary school years. So many skills to be mastered—all the basic equipment for every area of later learning and work. So much to learn about themselves and other people: how to make friends, how to stand up for oneself, how to join with others, how to be a team-mate, the meaning of sportsmanship; physical skills of all kinds; tremendous amounts of factual information; an awareness of individual strengths and weaknesses—what one can do easily and well, what makes hard work, what kinds of things just aren't within one's scope at all; so much to learn about one's community, about one's government, about the world.

A lot of nice, intelligent, talented kids are going to have learning problems they never would have had if they had been born twenty years earlier. A lot of hard-working kids are going to fail courses that no one would ever have made them take, even ten years ago. . . . There just never was a time when competition was this great; the population explosion, the need for more highly skilled people, the rapid decline of semi-skilled and unskilled jobs, require that many more of the already greatly increased population go on to college. Some of our children will have to take some courses over. Some will have to study during the summers. Some will have to have tutoring—not because they are any dumber than we were but because the world presents them with tougher competition. If we are clear about this we can relieve a lot of unnecessary anxiety and circumvent unnecessary feelings of failure.

* *The Under-Achiever* The expression "under-achiever" first came into use primarily in connection with the bright child who was unable to learn because of some psychological block. It was a useful concept insofar as it was used in a

*From *The Conspiracy Against Childhood*. Pages 62–68, line 25.

protective and compassionate way to help parents and teachers understand that there were times in the lives of some children when they simply could not function successfully in intellectual pursuits because they were too preoccupied with some emotional disturbance. It was certainly a more useful descriptive term than "lazy," "ornery" or "stupid."

Unfortunately, as our educational demands and expectations have increased, the term "under-achievement" has too often come to take on an entirely different meaning; it now describes any child who is not doing the level of work that adults arbitrarily assign to him. As a result many of today's "under-achievers" are yesterday's normal children; if they had been lucky enough to be born fifty or more years ago, they would have been considered quite competent in terms of some of the things they know that we now take for granted. Many of the children we now label as "not living up to their potential" have more information than their grandfathers had when they were adults.

In the mad rush for academic acceleration more and more nice, normal kids, are being labeled as under-achievers or failures without regard for the change in our expectations. We turn our schools into failure factories, insist that our children grow up according to an entirely new time schedule, demand a much higher level of achievement from nursery school to college—and then wonder why so many intelligent children cannot "live up to their potential!" Whose potential? What kind of potential? A potential for memorizing? A potential for sitting at a desk and doing homework for two hours in sixth grade? A potential for taking tests well?

In order to understand what is labeled as under-achievement in school performance we need to examine how the world of school looks to our children. First of all, it is a world of absolutes, of success or failure. We are not asking our children to do their own best but to be *the* best. Education is in danger of becoming a religion based on fear; its doctrine is to compete. The majority of children are being led to believe that they are doomed to failure in a world which has room only for those at the top.

There seems to be a new theory in education—one which I do not believe has appeared before—that everything we learn in every field of endeavor must be learned by everybody. We have made so much progress in scientific knowledge in such a short time—more in the last 100 years than in all human history—that it has simply overwhelmed us and seems to have robbed us of good sense and good judgment; in fact, the whole notion that we have to teach every child all that we know is sheer nonsense. I have grown up during an era in which the radio, TV, the airplane, penicillin, the theory of relativity, and the splitting of the atom have been invented and developed. I understand nothing of consequence about any of them. I leave the navigating of a plane to the pilot, my doctor decides when I need penicillin and there is a radio and TV repairman at the corner. Most of us who are now adults have lived through a period of unbelievable change. How has it affected those of us who are now over forty? We have all remained specialists; we have learned what we needed to know for our own work; we have learned that part of the total knowledge available that interested us. And though we do not know a great deal about almost everything, we do not feel stupid, incompetent or handicapped. When we need to know something we look it up or ask somebody or get some books or take a course—but at no time do we feel that the great force of all the new scientific knowledge must weigh on each of us personally. And it is important to remember that it *is* quite specifically scientific knowledge which has advanced so rapidly—not greater understanding of ourselves, not the ability to live more intelligently with others, not the finding new and better ways of solving human problems.

If our get-tough approach in education were to produce a generation of intellectual giants or creatively gifted human beings one might concede at least an opportunistic justification, if not a moral one. But there is every reason to believe that the current approach is *not* a sound method for helping children develop the best they have to offer.

One of our major difficulties is that we have tended to equate intelligence with creativity, as though they were interchangeable. Recent studies indicate that nothing could be further from the truth. Typical of many such reports is that of Dr. Emmy E. Werner, Assistant Professor of Child Development at the University of California. She stated that a number of studies revealed that only about one third of the children from nursery through high school could be regarded as highly creative and highly intelligent as measured by intelligence tests and academic performance. More frequently there was a difference of about 25 I.Q. points, creative children performing at the lower level on I.Q. tests. She reported that children who were judged in these studies as being highly creative were frequently regarded by their teachers as having wild or silly ideas and as being less ambitious, hard-working, and studious than the high-I.Q. children. In an article in the *Nursery Education Journal,* Dr. Werner wrote: "When we contrast youngsters who are gifted in the traditional sense— those with a high I.Q.—with children who score high on tests of creative thinking, we find one group seems to be better at finding the one right, recognized answer (convergent thinking) and that the other excels in thinking that takes off in new directions (divergent thinking)."

*The Test Marathon*  Nowhere does our collective madness about education show up more blatantly than in relation to tests and grades. The specter of tests hangs over the heads of our children like a nightmare, haunting them from nursery school to graduate school. Phyllis McGinley described this atmosphere: "Tests sort them, classify them, winnow them out as if they were gradable peas from a commercial garden."

At the heart of the matter is the intelligence test, and just as with the description "under-achiever," so too the term

65

"intelligence quotient" or "I.Q." started out to be a means of communicating about children with special problems. Binet and Simon, who devised the first intelligence test, never dreamed that they were creating such a Frankenstein; Simon said as much a few years ago. Their original purpose was to design a test that could help the classroom teacher discover cases of mental retardation and check the general abilities of the students. They spoke of it as a "minor tool," as an adjunct and a check on the teacher's personal observations and judgments, its primary purpose being to identify children who might need special help.

The test was based on a relatively simple design; for example, a large number of children, all ten years old, are asked to answer a question. If 50 percent can answer it, the question is considered reasonable for ten-year-olds. Numbers of such tests or questions involving information, reasoning, memory and various kinds of manual and perceptual skills are assigned to every age group on this basis, resulting in an examination in which at any given age level 50 percent will get a score below 100 and 50 percent will get above 100. In other words, there is set up an arbitrary division of the entire population in order to find an average. The Intelligence Quotient is obtained by dividing the "Mental Age" (a child's score on the test) by his chronological age and multiplying by 100. If the mental age is higher than the chonological age, the score will be above 100; if the mental age is lower than the chronological age, the score will be below 100. The main point to remember is that *50 percent of the population must get 100 or below*—that is how the test is designed.

It is absolutely essential to remember that I.Q. scores are frequently very poor predictors. Even within the limits of their usefulness they are often incorrect. When I first started practicing to administer intelligence tests most of my subjects got scores which seemed to indicate that they were feebleminded. As I learned to use the tool better it was amazing how much smarter all of the children of the students and professors at the college became where I was taking a course in testing. An experienced, warm and generally approving examiner gets higher scores from his subjects than do inexperienced examiners or one who finds it difficult to relate easily to his subjects. If the examiner has been told that he is testing mentally retarded children, or exceptionally bright children, his expectations may play a subtle and unconscious role in the test results.

In the original conception intelligence tests were not viewed as suitable for group administration. Except in special cases where an extensive individual evaluation is felt to be needed, group intelligence tests are now administered by many schools. Given individually it was possible for the examiner to view the test results in relation to an individual child's level of anxiety; confusions and misinterpretations of questions could be noted. Even important variables, such as whether or not a child seemed to be tired or was getting a cold or tended to be shy with a stranger, could be incorporated into the evaluation of the results. We are faced therefore with a double problem in group testing; there is no opportunity for these observations, and as testing has gained in importance, children taking them tend to become more nervous and uneasy about them. The child with a consistent tendency to become flustered by testing situations is often penalized unfairly.

With such masses of children to educate, with the inevitable necessity for some means of assessing readiness for each new level of schooling, we must rely on tests to some degree. Especially in such a mobile society, where families move from one place to another, it is necessary to find some relatively rapid way of placing children into new school systems. Used with discretion tests can be a convenient and reasonably efficient way to handle some of the Herculean tasks of mass education. But we will defeat these sensible purposes if we worship tests results, viewing them as final answers or as having a mystical validity handed down by God.

Grades and report cards are also notoriously poor at predicting future success; scratch almost any "famous" person, and you will find that somewhere, tucked away for safekeeping and brought out for an occasional self-satisfied chuckle on a rainy evening, is a well-preserved packet of neatly tied *terrible* report cards! On a somewhat more scientific basis, a research report which reviewed forty-six studies dating back to 1917 of the relationship between college grades and later success in a variety of careers, led the author, Donald P. Hoyt, to the conclusion: "Present evidence strongly suggests that college grades bear little or no relationship to any measure of adult accomplishment."

Despite such observations parents tend to view report cards with a "this is it" attitude; notwithstanding all that they may know about the children they live with twenty-four hours a day that may be contrary to the report card's evaluation, they accept it as *the verdict*. Not only is such an approach unsound but considering the difficulties the human race has always had in communicating with each other, written report cards tend to be misinterpreted unless there is a direct contact between the parent and the teacher. And once we have instituted this person-to-person relationship the report card becomes unnecessary.

*The Influence of a Great Teacher*  Most of what goes on in our schools today is regimented rote learning of an odd assortment of facts. Too many of our children are made to feel like failures before third grade—and by the time they are in high school and college, they are old cynics who see no relevance between what they are forced to digest and memorize and what is meaningful to them. They are fully aware of the double standard that says they must show competence in all areas while adults are not only allowed, but encouraged to develop their own unique and special strengths.

It is impossible to go into any detail about the wide split between sound educational philosophy and the painful reality which faces our children in today's schools. It does seem to me that as we send our children back to school there is a question we can ask ourselves that may help us to understand what our children are going through and which will make it possible for us to be their compassionate allies when the going gets rough—when they are struggling with too much homework and impossible exams that none of us could pass, and with the necessity to study subjects in depth that interest them not the slightest, and that will have no constructive bearing whatsoever on their adult lives.

The question is, who were the teachers you remember as having played a significant part in what was of most value to you, during your school years? Was it the teachers who knew the most about the subject they were teaching? Or was it rather those teachers who loved *teaching?*

Such teachers cannot bring their love of life and learning to fulfillment in classes of thirty or forty students. They cannot share their wonder, they cannot create a climate of adventure in a classroom where everything they teach must come out of a syllabus. They cannot become the loving friends they want to be when they are forced to give daily, weekly, monthly examinations, and a grade at the end of the course that measures nothing of the slightest consequence about personal development and growth, but simply lines every one up in relation to some arbitrary norm of achievement.

As parents who remain on the outside looking in, it isn't enough to be grateful for our advanced years—our escape into the safety of adulthood. Our beautiful children, with all those treasures and possibilities within them, need our help in understanding that *they* are not failing but that their education is to be challenged. And those special, those *good*

69

teachers—the ones that our children will someday remember with such love—need all the support we can give them to change the schools.

*A Proposal to Teach Reading in the Third Grade*    There is probably no educational controversy that rages more wildly than the question of when children ought to be taught to read. At one extreme are the people who say we are wasting valuable time if we let our kids just lie around, growing—that we ought to start teaching reading at ten months or even earlier. Some of the more conservative members of this group suggest waiting until two, when one can proceed to teach typing at the same time.

At the other extreme are the experts who tell us that all sorts of terrible things can happen if we start reading too early. There is research that suggests that if a child tries to begin to coordinate his eyes in order to recognize letters and words before his eye muscles can really handle this (sometimes as late as six or seven), he may well become a one-eyed reader. Neurologists tell us that there is such variation in neurological development that there may be an age span of two or more years in the physiological maturity of first-graders. Educators report that an individual child may show as much as a three- or four-year age span in different kinds of maturation—that a seven-year-old may have the mental ability of a nine-year-old, the social sophistication of a four-year-old, and the physical coordination of a six-year-old. These variations in growth rates mean that some children may be reading in kindergarten while others may not be ready until second grade or later. A recent investigation of the Gesell Institute reported their conclusion that 50 percent of the children now entering first grade are not mature enough to achieve what is expected of them.

It would be nice not to have to become partisan about the two extreme points of view. It would be nice to live in a world

* From *Natural Parenthood*. Pages 70–81.

where each child was deemed to be a new discovery—an uncharted sea, where no one tried to impose external rules and regulations, but where we watched the *child,* instead, and while providing him with a loving and stimulating environment let him tell *us* when he was ready. But such good sense seems quite remote, and during this period when the pushers are in the ascendancy, I have decided to take a position about as far at one end of the scale as I can get.

I propose that no child be *permitted* to learn to read until third grade—that teachers in kindergarten to second grade be instructed to thwart any evidence of a child's disobeying this rule. In this way every kid who is ready to read, somewhere between three and seven, will have to learn on the sly, by himself. He'll have to sneak books under the covers and learn by flashlight. When he goes to the public library he'll have to stand on tiptoe and lie about his age, making reading just about the most exciting pastime ever invented. The advantage to all this is that teaching *oneself* to read is far superior to being taught. This should be perfectly obvious because children teach themselves to speak with almost no failures. Have you ever heard of a child flunking talking? The percentage is negligible compared to school records on teaching reading where failures sometimes outnumber successes.

Furthermore, those children who are not ready to read until seven or eight would not become second-class citizens. Under my plan a child could even get to be eight years old without feeling that he is a hopeless moron who will never learn anything. It is possible that without having to worry about learning to read most children will develop remarkable and outstanding talents that would never have emerged if they were struggling with letters. Under my proposal by the time a child got around to reading he might already have become an amateur astronomer, a happy ornithologist, a singer or poet—or so enthusiastic about all there is to learn that he will be a successful schoolboy before he can even spell cat. His teachers would be on their toes, too, having to keep up

71

with a wide and exciting assortment of interests while reading to children. Having had several years for running and jumping, such children will probably be ready for sitting still, too.

There he is now—shiny and bright-eyed and eight years old—shall his teacher teach him to read? Not on your life. Teachers have been too corrupted by reading theories; they tend to be fanatics of one kind or another, some believing in the religion of phonetics, others seduced by one or another of the overpriced systems planned for them by psychologists who have had very little contact with children. The ones to teach the third-graders ought to be the sixth-graders—and not necessarily the best readers. There is a good deal of evidence to suggest that the best reading teachers are children having trouble learning to read themselves—they can pick up the trouble spots faster! They also tend to be quite compassionate and there can be one teacher for every student—an excellent arrangement.

*Goofing Off*   Each year as summertime rolls around I find myself wanting to speak out in favor of goofing-off! It seems to me that today's children, from cradle to college, are spending almost all their waking hours doing something useful, getting ahead, achieving all kinds of self-improvement goals. There is too little time for fun for its own sake and for inner contemplation. One of my favorite people, Christopher Robin, explained it to Pooh this way: "What I like *doing* best is *nothing*. It means just going along listening to all the things you can't hear and not bothering."

Let me say at once that I am all for creative pursuits, for stimulating and meaningful experiences that serve to enrich a child's life, make him feel more competent, and give him a sense of mastery over himself and his environment. But it seems to me that we have forgotten the kind of climate in which genuine growth takes place. We are in too much of a rush; we have put too much faith in busy-ness, as if this were the measure of internal progress.

72

The pressures on our children during the school year seem to be increasing by geometric progression—and because this is so it seems to me that one important ingredient we ought to provide during the summer months is time to do nothing. Many parents feel uneasy when a child seems to have nothing to do. They nag when a twelve-year-old sits indoors reading on a sunny day; they get fidgety when a five-year-old spends the morning tossing pebbles into a puddle. What we might well be more concerned about is the child who cannot bear it when left to his own devices, challenged to use his own inner resources. Doing nothing is really doing a lot. It is time to rest, to think one's own thoughts. Just "fooling around" is really a way in which we refill the reservoir of our inner life.

Several years ago I gathered together some comments of children about what they would like to do during the summer months. One youngster wrote, "I'd like to take a real long hike alone, lasting all summer. At times I might take a boat out on a lake for a couple of days and catch a lot of fish. . . . You would never believe that what I'm really doing this summer is going to a camp with an hour-by-hour schedule." Another child wrote, "My perfect summer vacation would be to live on a desert island for two months. I would like to have a little house with one door and a fireplace and a television set. The island would have palm trees and monkeys. All day I would play with the monkeys."

It would be foolish and destructive to suggest that summertime could or should be a vacuum—limitless time in which children have no stimulation from the environment, no opportunities to increase their sense of accomplishment. But whether a child goes to a camp or a play group, or whether he travels, he can be provided with some free time with an opportunity for the necessary pleasures of childhood—private explorations, lazy dreaming, a chance to feel at home in the natural world of sea and sky, sun and grass, insects and animals, whether in a city park playground, at the beach, or

73

at some plush resort. It isn't a waste of time; it is a necessary interval for refreshing one's soul.

Another child writing about his wishes for summer put it succinctly when he said, "A perfect summer is doing what you want to do without fighting for it. Think about it! All day, not being bossed by parents, lying on the couch sipping lemonade. Freedom, that's the best!"

I am myself refreshed by the image of this unbossed creature, supine with his lemonade. At the first opportunity, I plan to take his advice!

*The Under-Deprived Child*   A health expert recently caused quite a commotion by suggesting that school bus transportation only be provided for children two or more miles from school. It was his thesis that the nation's children would be in far better physical shape if they had to walk to school and that at least 50 percent of the chauffering now being done by parents was unnecessary coddling.

At first glance one is inclined to think of these nonwalking children as overprivileged; in one sense they are—there is too much *car* in their lives. But in another sense they are deprived —of the robust good health and the feelings of freedom and independence that might well come from doing more of their locomoting on their own. In other words, many of our most privileged children are under-deprived: given too many *things* they have little opportunity to experience some of the important feelings and events that are essential to healthy maturation.

Under-deprived youngsters rarely if ever know the exquisite joy of waiting for something, of anticipating and dreaming, nor do they discover the pride in working for a difficult goal on their own.

One mother reported that she recently went through the horrors of spring cleaning in her adolescent daughter's room. "I suddenly saw clearly how lack of 'deprivation' can give a child such a false sense of values. In that room there was a broken sewing machine; it had been bought by doting grand-parents for a twelfth birthday and had been used for making one dress and then never used again. There was a guitar bought over a year ago and accompanied by a year's lessons with an excellent teacher. When the teacher moved away and one string broke it was never played again. A record player had needed a new needle for several months and was gather-ing dust on the closet floor next to a typewriter given as a Christmas gift two years before, when my daughter swore that she needed one desperately for her school work. She had never taken the trouble to learn to use it. Then there was the newest acquisition, a tape recorder, left uncovered, the tapes scrambled in complete disorder.

"I found myself feeling sick at the waste, furious at my child, and suddenly aware of how foolish I had been to per-mit this. We aren't rich people and the money for all these luxuries could have been used for other needs. Even if we had been millionaires we should never have let our daughter develop such bad attitudes toward possessions. I began to wonder how she would ever stand the normal frustrations of life as an adult when she had almost never waited for any-thing she wanted as a child."

Several years ago a leading psychiatrist stated that one rea-son for the increasing number of very early marriages among middle-class youngsters while still in college (to say nothing of earlier sexual experimentation) was that we seemed to be in the process of raising a generation who never quite gave up demand feeding. From birth these children were taught that they never had to wait for the fulfillment of any gratification —they had a right to anything they wanted when they wanted it. While self-demand feeding may be appropriate in infancy our apparent adaptation of this concept to much later periods of growth has deprived our children of the normal and real-istic experiences of frustration, of struggle, of waiting for— and enjoying more—the fruits of responsible labor.

Certainly we cannot blame under-deprivation of our chil-

75

dren on the affluent society; wealthy families throughout history have often been the most stern and demanding with their children. Is it our own memories of the Depression? Are we giving our children things that were denied us? Is it part of our confusion about values and standards in facing the complexities and anxieties of the world we live in? Is it in part a lazy abdication from making demands or having expectations that involve enduring our children's disapproval and anger? Undoubtedly it is many things but we had better take note of what we are doing. We are keeping our children in cotton batting both physically and emotionally.

Our misguided wish to give more than is needed in material possessions means that we give less of what is *really* needed—an opportunity to behave responsibly and earn one's own self-respect. Our young people crave such experiences—and when they cannot tell us so as directly it is up to us as adults to control our impulses to be overgenerous and overprotective. We need to "deprive" our children of those things that interfere with healthy struggle and challenge. We need to have enough faith and self-discipline to permit our children to grow up.

*Children and Chores* High on the list of any discussion about what bothers parents most about their children's behavior is their attitudes toward chores. "How do you get a nine-year-old to put his pajamas away?" one mother will ask—and twenty others will laugh ruefully with immediate sympathy and understanding. Another mother will get the same response when she says, "Honestly, I think we ask so little of our kids—and no matter how I nag or threaten or punish, it's a war everytime I ask Peter to straighten up his room or put dirty underwear and towels into the hamper." There is immediate and vociferous agreement that our children are spoiled, lazy, irresponsible, and uncooperative about the simplest chores no matter how intense and forceful our efforts to produce more acceptable behavior may be.

76

But after all that is said and done I think we are still more uneasy than parents before us; there is something new and different about our concern. We are really worrying about the larger issue of what work means in the lives of our children. The nature and meaning of work have changed so profoundly in our own lives that we aren't at all sure what we want to teach our children about it. Much of our discomfort about their attitudes toward work reflects our own confusion and uncertainty about the social forces which have so dramatically affected our own attitudes toward it.

Ruminating about all this one night at the dinner table I asked our teen-age daughter what she thought about work. Her immediate and unhesitating reply was "Work should be fun and interesting." She startled me; would any generation before hers have thought of work primarily in relation to fun? In any previous generation the spontaneous response to any question about work would have been, "Work? Why that's how we stay alive!" Just that simple and uncomplicated—a matter of survival. We are facing the serious and challenging question of how to interpret the meaning of work to our children during a period of such rapid social change that we are no longer at all sure ourselves what work really means.

Many of us who are now raising our own children are old enough to remember when dirty clothing was boiled in an enormous pot on the stove, when oatmeal had to cook overnight, and when baby foods had to be strained by hand every day. In such a world nobody really had to teach a child lessons about work; he was born into a world of shared work and he knew almost before he could walk that he was a *needed* worker. This is a world that we may remember only dimly but it is a world our children never saw at all; and we are faced with a dilemma never dreamed of by our ancestors; how do you get the children to help with the chores when they know darn well we don't *really need* them?

Our notions about work have also changed in relation to the educational expectations we have for our children. Up

77

until the past fifty years formal academic schooling was not nearly as important as it is today. Most of the survival skills had to do with learning crafts—learning to *do* more than learning to *know*. A child who could learn to make shoes or build boats or milk cows could have a feeling of worth and a hopeful view of his future; he could do something of value. The sixteen-year-old girl who went into the garment factory and learned to run a sewing machine didn't feel like a second-class citizen if she had only an eighth-grade education. In today's labor market we have no room for early "doers"; we require all our children, whether or not they are so constituted, to become thinkers and knowers. If some of our children seem lazy and unmotivated it may be partly because they were born in the wrong century—for them! If we find it difficult to interest our offspring in making their beds and putting away their toys and clothes it may be that we are underestimating the kinds of pressures with which they live. It may be true that our children are lucky that we are enlightened enough not to permit them to work as juvenile slaves in mines and factories, but we are kidding ourselves if we think our children are not often enslaved in new ways. How many of our children would prefer to go to work than to battle the New Math or struggle through examinations until they are twenty!

Household chores must still be done whether or not they are matters of life or death. We could probably save a lot of time and energy if we were to acknowledge how dull and boring we find these tasks—but how much we enjoy the end results. With this orientation we are better equipped to answer our children when they say "What for?" when we ask them to put away their toys or straighten out the record cabinet in the living room. The answer can be honest and realistic; it is to give us all a comfortable, attractive place in which to do the things we enjoy doing. However, we need to be clearer in or own minds about what necessity really means in our homes. How often do we demand a kind of perfection in orderliness that really has little or nothing to do with this goal of comfort? Aren't there many tasks that could be eliminated or modified?

We might, on occasion, sit down with our children and talk to them about what *they* think is needed. Maybe they think the dog needs a longer run in the back yard or they need a more spacious shed for outdoor toys; maybe they have some practical ideas for creating more shelf space in the playroom or building a desk-top that can be folded up against the wall to save space in their bedroom. We might all discuss together how these important-to-them projects can be carried out, for they will learn far more about the real meaning of work by what makes sense to them than by simply carrying out our orders for things *we* think are important.

We need to be careful that we don't interfere too much in those jobs that our children do, but imperfectly. Too often we fill in when a child does something that doesn't live up to our higher standards so he can't feel any genuine sense of accomplishment. A four-year-old dusts the dining room table, shows it to us with pride, and while we are saying "That's lovely, darling," we are absentmindedly finishing the job to our satisfaction. Part of learning to enjoy work is to be permitted to execute and complete it to our satisfaction not someone else's. When seven-year-old Debbie makes you an apron with one fat tie and one skinny tie, that's the way it ought to stay if we want her to go on to other pleasures in sewing-all-by-yourself.

Some drudgery falls into the most glamorous of lives—this is a fact about household chores that must be accepted and tolerated. Our children need to understand that you can't love what you are doing all of the time. Some things just have to be done in order to reach a goal. For a three-year-old this may mean, "If we clean up your toys together we will have time for a story." For a five-year-old it may mean, "If you put your bicycle in the garage every night it won't get rusty." For a nine-year-old it may mean, "If you help me with my chores—save me some time by watering the lawn—I'll be able to drive you down to the high school football game on Saturday."

What we have to communicate to our children is that cooperation is good human relations and that this is just as important as it ever was. We need to be clear in our own minds that there is no inborn instinct that will drive a child to shoulder responsibilities that annoy or bore him. It wasn't strength of character that drove great-grandpa to the wood-pile after school every day—it was the sure knowledge that there would be cold winter nights if he didn't do his job. We can't pretend with our children that what we ask of them is nearly so vital but we can make it clear that sharing what has to be done, however unexciting the jobs may be, is an expression of love and a sure road to self-respect.

Even young children can begin to discover that meaningful work has to do with personal fulfillment not necessarily with monetary considerations. But if work has more to do today with personal development this implies that we must give children a sense that they are working for their own goals, not for ours. Work used to be for one's parents; many of us grew up in an era when we can remember very well that we thought a great deal more about pleasing our parents than ourselves. I think we want our children to work hard for what *they* will gain from their own accomplishments, and we have to make some clear distinctions about this to our children.

We need to help our children see that we do not think of work in a narrow way, as only being related to how one earns one's livelihood. We can each find those work activities that stretch our talents and that serve others, that fire the imagination and that make us feel needed. The essential quality in this view of work is that it can take many forms, vocational and avocational, but that it is important to find work that one needs for self-respect and personal fulfillment.

With less time needed to devote to household chores there

will be time for useful work in the communities in which we live and creative work on our own; there is honorable and pleasurable work for all of us to do that makes us feel good, that gives us a sense of well-being and pride in our accomplishments. Children can begin to feel needed for the contributions they can make. In one family a two-dollar contribution is made to UNICEF everytime a child mows the lawn. In another, a teen-ager is relieved of all dishwashing because he gives two afternoons a week to teaching children to read in a special volunteer teaching program in a deprived neighborhood. In still another household all major household cleaning is done by the whole family on Saturday mornings so that Mother and her two youngsters can have the free time during the week to take ceramics and dancing classes.

There has never been a time when young people had more scope, more variety of opportunities to find the work that will be meaningful and fulfilling. Our children can realistically expect to find work that they will enjoy doing—there is nothing sinful or immoral in that! Sometimes it will be the work they do to earn a living, sometimes it will be the work they do that has nothing to do with earning a living; the important thing will be knowing that to be most truly and joyously alive one must work. To conclude, I think my daughter was right —in today's world it is reasonable to assume that most of one's work *can* be fun and interesting! I think we ought to accept our children's orientation toward work in these terms —but we must help them to see this in its broadest meaning; fun is when you feel challenged to do your best, when somebody needs you, and when you are proud of what you are doing.

# TOPICS FOR PARENT MEETINGS
## AND DISCUSSION GROUPS

The programs dealing with the school-age child on *How Do Your Children Grow?* were given the following titles:

1. "Help! We are the parents of a wave-fighter!"
   (Individual constitutional differences in children's reactions to real-life challenges. Differences in coping techniques.)
2. "But tell me, teacher, will more facts save the world?"
   (Providing children with lots of facts makes them neither wise nor good human beings. The basic misconceptions in modern educational practices, about what learning is all about. The difference between cleverness and intellectual excellence. Academic pressures, emphasis on rote learning.)
3. "You forgot to schedule time for dreaming."
   (The development of inner resources, a rich inner life, as against just being very busy all the time. The over-scheduled child.)
4. "How do you make a conscience?"
   (Punishments and rewards, helping children to develop inner controls. Identification with parental values through love. Discipline.)
5. "Remember when kids could be kids and rob apples from orchards?"
   (Children and the law; the ever-increasing degree to which social controls come not from family and neighbors, but from the police. Decreasing tolerance of "childish pranks," as cities become more crowded, more impersonal, less able to provide genuine adventures for children. Too much supervision and over-protection. Changing attitudes of what we tolerate in children's behavior.)
6. "How much will you pay me for making my bed?"
   (Chores, allowances, work responsibilities.)
7. "Let's civilize up around here!"
   (Parents' rights, maintaining standards of behavior, the value and importance of humor in dealing with the grade-

school child. Problem of parental toleration for age-appropriate behavior.)

In general, during these seven sessions, parents of school-age children discussed these major areas;

Chores, work, allowances, responsibilities, over-indulgence

Discipline—punishments and rewards

Anger—and what to do about it

Social development—shyness, influence of the peer group, unnatural acceleration in parties, etc.

Gradual loss of total parental controls—growing awareness of parents' "clay feet."

Neatness, sloppiness, rudeness, curiosity

Energy level—wildness, restlessness, fidgeting, squirming— need for adventure, for not sitting still all day, for less supervised activities, less over-protection.

Academic pressures, achievement, marks, grades, tests

Increasing demands for more freedom vs. regressions to infantile behavior

Individual differences in growth, unevenness in growth

Need for new types of affection and support

Conscience, identification with parents

Reactions and concerns about social issues—what children worry about—smoking, drugs, war, safety in the streets, race relations

Verbal pseudo-sophistication vs. emotional immaturity

Emphasis on college as a goal. Comes earlier and earlier.

Stealing

Competition

Recreation and vacations

Can a parent make mistakes and apologize? Meaning of respect for authority.

Over-loading of extra-curricular activities (music lessons)

City living—anonymity, mobility of families, indifference of adults to child's behavior or problems, in the streets.

# SUPPLEMENTARY RESOURCES

*Monologues for Parents of Grade-School Children*

*Everything Will Be Fine* by Judith Menken. Starting school, achievement, pressures, homework, parent-teacher relations at 1st grade level. Nassau County Mental Health Assoc., 186 Clinton St., West Hempstead, New York, 50¢.

*Let's Go Shopping* by Judith Menken. Conflict of values between parent and child, how much parental control over clothes, allowance, etc. Same source and price.

*When I Was Your Age* by Judith Menken. Friendship relationships and parental feelings as child struggles in relationships with peers. Same source and price.

*Plays For Parents of Grade-School Children*

*It Doesn't Grow on Trees* by Ernest Kinoy. Family hang-ups about money, allowances, over-indulgence, parental extravagance, etc. (Written with great humor by a well known TV writer.) 3 parts. Nassau County Mental Health Assoc., 186 Clinton St., West Hempstead, New York, 50¢.

*Random Target* by Nora Stirling. One of the best mental health plays ever written, deals with discipline and feelings of hostility. Mental Health Materials Center.

*Who Takes Out the Garbage?* by Sadie Hofstein. Responsibility, chores, father-mother relationship. Funny and very true to life.

*Films For Parents of Grade-School Children*

*And So They Grow* 28 min. Produced for The Play Schools Association, and deals with a recreation program under their leadership. An excellent example of how much children learn through play—the film makes it quite clear that the children are learning more, in many ways, than they do in the regular school hours. Useful for discussion of goals in education, how children learn. Rental information, Campus Films, 14 E. 53rd St., New York, N.Y., 10022.

*Angry Boy* 33 min. Mental Health Film Board. An old film but a classic. First rate examination of hidden hostility, stealing, the meaning of behavior, needs of children, the services of mental health clinics, parental fear and guilt. New York

University Film Library, 29 Washington Square, New York, N.Y.

*Parent to Child About Sex* 30 min. General discussion of the issues of sex education. Two rental sources, Yeshiva Univ. New York, N.Y., $20. Wayne State Univ., A-V Center, Detroit, Mich.

*Sibling Relations and Personality* 22 min. McGraw-Hill. Good springboard for discussion of how role in family may or may not influence personality development. New York Univ. Film Library.

*Pamphlets And Books*

*A Child Development Point of View* by James Hymes, Prentice Hall, 1955.

*Common Sense in Teaching Reading* by Roma Gans. Bobbs-Merrill, 1963.

*Crisis in the Classroom: The Remaking of American Education* by Charles E. Silberman. Random House, 1970.

*Don't Push Me!* Assoc. for Childhood Ed. Internat'l, 3615 Wisconsin Ave. N.W., Washington, D.C., 20016. 75¢.

*Helping Brothers and Sisters to Get Along* by Helen Puner, Child Study Assoc., 9 E. 89th St. New York, N.Y. 10028. 70¢.

*How Children Fail* by John Holt, Pitman, 1964.

*How Children Learn* by John Holt, Pitman, 1967.

*Kindergarten: A Year of Learning* by Marguerita Rudolph and Dorothy Cohen, Appleton, 1964.

*Pre-Adolescents: What Makes Them Tick?* By Fritz Redl, Child Study Assoc.

*The Children Are Dying* by Nat Hentoff. Viking, 1966.

*The Lives of Children* by George Denison, Random House, 1969.

*Understanding Your Child* by James L. Hymes, Prentice Hall, 1952.

*The Why and How of Discipline* by Aline Auerbach. Child Study Assoc.

*Your Child's Sense of Responsibility* by Edith Neisser. Public Affairs Pamphlets, same source and price.

*What to Tell Your Child About Birth, Death, Illness, Di-*

85

*vorce and Other Crises* by Helene Arnstein, Pocket Books, 1 W. 39th St. New York, N.Y. 10018. 60¢.
*What to Tell Your Child About Sex* Child Study Association, for address, 50¢.

# Chapter IV

## THE YEARS OF ROOTS AND WINGS
### The Teen-Age Years

* Parental fears and anxieties reach an all-time high during their children's adolescence. For one thing parents say that they find it very hard to talk to their children, that an alienation seems to set in, and at a time when one might think verbal communication ought to be getting easier it is far more difficult. Parents also say that they are frequently upset by their children's criticisms of them—that too often adolescents hit the target in assessing parental weaknesses and failures. Consciously or unconsciously many parents find this age a special strain, for just as they begin to feel that their own youth and vigor is on the wane and are regretting what they have not done with their own lives, they are faced with children who have it all ahead of them and who are filled with promise. There may be jealousy of youth's vitality, its ascendant sexuality, of the opportunities in the future. Parents also feel that crucial choices and decisions must be made in the next few years and that mistakes now may be more serious or at least more significant. The psychological flight of children is accentuated and dramatized when they leave home for college, and parents are faced with an intense awareness of how their own lives will be changed. There are

* From *How to Survive Parenthood*. Pages 87–90, line 24.

of course great differences between twelve- and fourteen-year-olds and between fifteen- and twenty-year-olds. But despite these differences it seems to me that a common enough thread or theme exists which is generally valid for these years of growth.

Living with adolescents can be so rough on one's ego that survival seems extremely unlikely some of the time! One of our handicaps at this stage of our children's growth is that somewhere along the line some of us got the idea that if we were good parents our children would love us all the time. If we are *really* good parents they will more likely think that they loathe us some of the time, and it is time we began to face the fact that it is *not* necessary to be loved by our children every minute—we simply must learn to tolerate their animosity. We cringe and shake with fright at being the targets of so much disapproval and rebellion. We are "understanding parents" and that means that we deserve to be loved! Because we are the most doting and over-indulgent parents in history our children's lack of gratitude is doubly unbearable and puzzling. It seems as though the more we give and try to understand the more they bite the outstretched hand!

But the worst part of this period is the sense of finality, especially during the later years of adolescence. Parents often feel that the "chips are down," and whatever we have or have not been able to accomplish in helping our children grow well to adulthood we must now accept as a *fait accompli*. Before going any further let me suggest that if you are the parent of a teen-ager and have been feeling this way, sit back and think for a moment about all the things that have happened to you since the age of twenty-one. What were the experiences that changed you? What have you learned and how did you learn it? Are you in any way, shape, or form the same person you were then? In all likelihood you are not. We can eliminate at least this one fear! The truth of the matter is that emotional growth can be far greater and more dramatic between twenty-one and sixty than before—despite what some psychiatrists may have been telling us!

We are afraid of the pseudo-sophistication of our thirteen- and fourteen-year-olds. Forgetting that their academic course work at school now involves mental gymnastics we once thought more appropriate to graduate school, we are frightened by other signs of acceleration. Our present generation of teen-agers is brighter, better informed, more articulate, more knowledgeable and has more psychological insight than any previous generation.

We seem too often to be providing *things* for young people instead of ideas, values, purpose, and the challenges and expectations that can give them dignity. It is immoral for a sixteen-year-old to be given a Mercedes Benz, or a twelve-year-old to be given two $25 bathing suits. Parents defend such indulgence on the grounds that we live in an affluent society and that it is silly to withhold what we can easily afford. They say it is natural to want to give to one's children. It is not natural at all. There have always been wealthy families but they have not always overindulged their children.

A high school principal said, "These kids have been robbed of the most important gift we should give them: the right to genuine experiences, a chance to be tested, to see what their strengths are. We keep them in cotton batting until they just go berserk trying to find *some* way to grow up."

We need to know this problem side of things, but of course it is only *one* side of the story. The other is (as you may have been impatiently acknowledging on your own) that for all the storm and stress, adolescence is also a marvelous time of life and the most wonderful things happen to our children! Whatever problems there may be, either in our bungling efforts to be helpful or in the world in which they find themselves, our children have youth and resilience on their side and a quite unbelievable capacity to snap back, no matter how great a crisis may be. Despite bravado, they are vulnerable and achingly sensitive; though parroting the materialistic chatter of their elders they are capable of idealism, fervor, and compassion. They have been exposed to cultural and cosmopolitan experiences so early in life that it often startles and unsettles us to hear them talk. Before the age of twenty, so many of our children have travelled extensively, feel at home all over the world, have eaten the foods, talked with the people and walked the streets of strange and utterly different places than home. Easier travel, television, paperback books, local community theaters, concerts, opera, have provided them with enormous riches unknown to young people before.

*The Communication Gap*   What then can we do about the problems and the potentials of our adolescents? First of all we should learn how to *talk* to them again! Stop being embarrassed and self-conscious just because *they* are; it is appropriate to be uncommunicative at seventeen not at forty-five. We shouldn't just sit back hopefully and say to ourselves, "I believe in my child"; we should tell our children what we think, what we believe to be right, and we should teach them ways to behave—and *then* we may give them many opportunities to try to test us and themselves, knowing they cannot (and really should not) be expected to accept our standards without resistance and experimentation.

 * There is clear evidence that young people want very much to remain in touch with parents and are eager for other adult models and guides as well. A genuine stumbling block to effective communications has to do with the profound complexities associated with the art of parental listening. Too often we say we will try to listen and try to learn if our children will do the same with us—if they will listen to what we have learned with age and experience. It sounds like a perfectly sensible and fair arrangement; it isn't. When we listen to our children we are staying young and alert, we are being

* From *Sex and Your Teen-Ager*. Pages 90–93, line 31.

helped to remain part of the mainstream of life. Trying to understand, to feel compassion, to increase our sensitivity to their problems and feelings, makes us feel good.

Listening to *us* makes *them* feel bad! Because we are their parents, listening means giving in, giving up; it means becoming our babies again, being infantilized. The act of listening is simply too dangerous. They have been listening to us for fifteen or more years—and whether we believe it or not they heard us very well! There is not a self-respecting 17-year-old extant who does not really know what his parents stand for, what they believe in, what matters to them. Listening has always been associated with obeying or rebelling—in either case, a reaction to authority.

Young people can listen to each other, they can listen to *other* adults, but it seems to me that for parents, one important step toward communication with one's *own* child is being willing to listen without always insisting on talking back! Sometimes *really* listening shifts the whole parent-child relationship enough so that eventually parental participation is welcomed again—even sought. It seems to me we can be most helpful to young people if we start out with the idea that we will really try to become good listeners. If we are honest about it we will probably realize that this is something we have never done very well.

I feel I can say this because it is so clearly something that I have failed at myself, so frequently! We sit down at the dining room table with a group of young people—and I feel myself preparing speeches, to defend my adult position on every topic they bring up! I forget we are just talking and that much of what they are saying is to test and shock me, and that they would not carry much of what they are saying into action.

At one discussion the young people took a position of such despair and anger that I started trying to balance the picture. They only went to greater extremes until I realized I was going to blow my top and left the table. A few minutes later my daughter came in to the kitchen and lovingly patted me on the head and said, "Poor Mommy—we scare the hell out of you, don't we!" I felt like an idiot. I went back and tried to practice what I preach to other parents! I asked questions, I suggested implications of what they were saying, I sympathized—also I *shut up and listened!* In a short time the tension in the atmosphere began to dissipate; we were no longer adversaries. The more I tried to understand and reflect what they felt, the more they were willing to wait to see what I wanted to say.

I am not suggesting that we ought to become self-conscious and unnatural in our discussions with our children. Only that we try to be honest enough to realize how terribly forceful and aggressive we usually are.

Because we haven't always been good listeners, and also simply because we are parents and we care so deeply and are so anxious, many of our teen-agers have seemed to develop an allergic reaction to almost all adults! They expect us to be judgmental and hostile and to interfere. There is almost a reflex action, if, for example, you accidentally bump into a teen-ager on a bus or a subway—there is a fury in the eyes that is painful to see. There is an involuntary defensiveness every time you open your mouth to express an opinion—the back goes up, escape is sought. We have a lot to undo! This generation of young people feel very deeply that they must make their own decisions and when they think that our attitude is only one of disapproval and lack of understanding they turn us off more completely than has probably ever been true before. You can't make an ally of someone who sees you as the enemy. It takes great patience and forbearance and great effort over a long period of time to re-establish lines of communication when this has happened.

*Parents No Matter What*   It is surely no service to our young people to hide our heads in the sand, to pretend we hear and see nothing. Total acceptance—"anything goes"—is as harmful as total disapproval.

We can make it clear that we are *always* available, ready to try to help, even when we may disapprove. We can be quite candid about our reservations and fears and at the same time that we indicate that we have respect for the young person's serious attempts to work out his own life. After doing everything possible to make our feelings quite clear we then must accept what we cannot change. Standing by its *not* approving—it is merely being loving.

We must certainly insist on having our feelings and sensitivities respected. On the other hand there is great value for us in trying to go on growing and changing, modifying our prejudices, broadening our viewpoint with changing times and circumstances. Not for our children's benefit but for our own—for unless we continue to grow and change our own lives become stultified and meaningless. Changes are never all bad; some make a great deal of sense and lead us in new and better directions.

We can try to convey in a general way what it means to be open to life, to accept all experiences as having significance, to love without fear of mistakes. Setbacks and failures are the necessary price for being fully and deeply alive. To accept growth and change is to have a dynamic view of life in which today's events may color the future but not limit it.

The essential ingredients for communication is trust—a genuine respect for the essential character of one's offspring. If we lack that by the time our children reach adolescence we are in more serious difficulty than we can handle without professional guidance. We ought to have no hesitancy about seeking that for ourselves and our children but we ought to be carefully discriminating—making sure that the help we find is the right help.

* *Drop-outs*   Like the term "under-achiever," "drop-out" must be viewed in the context of the times we live in.

* From *The Conspiracy Against Childhood*. Pages 93–96, line 30.

In our current hysteria about education, with our excessive devotion to standardization, we seem to have decided that anyone who drops out of school is a failure, running *from* a situation rather than running *toward* another. Characteristic of this point of view is a Public Affairs Pamphlet entitled "School Failures and Drop Outs," which states, "In general it is the relatively stable youngsters who cope with the school's program and the relatively unstable, whose scholastic attainments tend to be poor, who leave." This refers to high-school drop-outs and the statistics are very convincing; it is perfectly true that particularly at the high-school level drop-outs tend to be those who are failing. The question is, however, *why* they are failing and *why* they leave. It seems to me that one legitimate answer is that the schools have failed in meeting the needs of these young people. For example, the pamphlet reports that many drop-outs "have a consuming desire for ready money for dates and cars." What is really so hard to understand about that? Put into the perspective of history 100 years ago *and in every other period of human history* most sixteen-year-olds *were* working and earning money; they were regarded by society as young adults who *should* be out on their own and making their way in the world. It would seem that judgments about an individual's goals depend more on the social context in which he lives, than on any intrinsically human qualities.

In our zeal to equate success with degrees there are a great many questions that we have failed to ask ourselves about school drop-outs. As holds true for the under-achievers there are some young people who are in serious trouble emotionally, for whom dropping out of school is merely a symptom of inner turmoil. There always have been such special problems and I do not believe that their numbers have increased, except insofar as the increase in external pressures may be contributing to their psychological burdens. But if we take a candid look at the experiences and the values that make up a large part of the high-school and college scene, it seems

94

to me we might well be inclined to call our drop-outs drop-*ins;* we have been too callous and too casual in our assumptions; drop-outs may very well be leaving something that is at best useless and at worst harmful while some times eagerly, often desperately, seeking for something better.

Some of our young people are so deeply affected by the incongruities, the hypocrisy, the shallowness of the life around them that their general disillusionment is expressed in a wish to rebel by escape. But we are making a mistake if we interpret this attitude merely as immaturity or instability. The world in which we live is *really* so cock-eyed that it doesn't seem to me at all surprising or alarming that so many young people are in such distress.

Not everyone should be expected to attend either the traditional high school or college; we must invent and find new and original approaches to education.

There is no reason to assume that the age of eighteen is the best time to go to college; in fact there is considerable evidence that it is *not* the most desirable time. The GI's who went to college after the Second World War with their wives and babies tended to be the best students the colleges had ever seen.

One of the reasons they give for leaving school and wanting to work as volunteers is that they need time "to find themselves," to discover what really interests them most. With individual life so long and with the likelihood that retirement will become increasingly a burden rather than a boon (sixty-five-year-olds today are just too vigorous and healthy to be put out to pasture), it seems to be not at all illogical to offer young people work opportunities and experiences at that point in their lives when they are most eager for direct experience and want most desperately to have some autonomy, some financial independence—and then seeing to it that institutions of higher learning are so set up that it will not only be possible but easy and convenient to continue one's studies while one is marrying, parenting and working for a living. If

95

one is likely to want to go on working at something until the age of seventy or eighty there seems little reason to be in such a rush to finish one's education by twenty or twenty-five.

There are ways and ways of encouraging young people to "stick it out." This view was expressed succinctly by one young man who said, "So long as my parents kept yelling about needing a degree to get a good job and earn a lot of money I was sure I was going to leave. But then I talked to my advisor; I told him I wanted to leave school so I could work in the slums and help people in trouble. He asked me what I had to offer them—what could I bring to them—and then he asked me if I wanted to bring myself as a mature, competent, trained person, or did I want to bring them *my* poverty—my problems and my weaknesses. I stayed in school." Some young people are leaving school because we have given them the wrong reasons for staying.

Another aspect of keeping young people in school is giving them credit for some of what they do outside of school. There are children who are failing in school but who are not failing in life; who earn money, who give service, who sing and play musical instruments, who dance, who paint and write poetry, who take care of younger children responsibly, who can cook and sew or build ham radio sets, who serve as volunteers in all kinds of capacities, who ought to be getting credit for all the things they are, and can do, beyond the walls of the school building.

The way to encourage young people to stay in school is really quite simple: to make the alternative unthinkable and unbearable. It means offering learning opportunities that are as full of life and significance as one can find anywhere.

\* *Those Blooming Flower Children* (*and Revolutionaries*)
I have felt it a privilege to have lived during the era of The Flower Children. They have been a civilizing force—a reminder of what is best and most human in all of us. They

\* From *Sex and Your Teenager*. Pages 96–99.

have been our conscience when we have sorely needed prodding. I am speaking of the best of them—the ones who listened to the values we taught and shocked us by living up to them.

There is no question that many young people who run away from home, drop out of school, begin to take drugs, are seriously disturbed and dangerously self-destructive. It hardly seems any wonder that the more fragile of our young people would fall by the wayside during an era of such turmoil and unrest. They desperately need our help not our judgment or rejection.

In the light of so much agony and pain-of-the-soul, the use of mind-expanding drugs, or drugs that somehow remove reality altogether, or change it enough to make it endurable, doesn't seem terribly surprising or illogical. That they may be seriously dangerous and destructive goes without saying—and there can be little argument about the need for controls. But it seems to me you have to be prepared to offer something better if you want to discourage such usage; you are required as a responsible adult to find out what unmet needs for feeling deeply or escaping from reality are being met by drug-taking and then you have to change the environment that produces such needs. As far as marihuana is concerned if we offer tobacco and cigarettes as a comparable substitute then the kids are right; except for the fact that they will be imprisoned and cigarette smokers won't they may very well have selected a less dangerous soporific than we.

The simple minded "let's lock 'em up, they're no damn good," which seems to be our program of choice at the moment is not a relevant or helpful answer to the fact that today's young people feel themselves to be caught in an impossible trap, where feelings are frowned upon, where they are expected to be performing robots full of useless information, and living lives, like so many of ours, of quiet desperation—small meaningless cogs in a vast, impersonal, nightmarish machine—a monumental technology which consumes human beings. A Harvard professor, Thomas J. Cottle, offers one explanation for the taking of drugs, in saying, "One senses an ironical and twisted searching for insanity." Which reminds one of the obvious truth that may lie behind such a search—Nietzsche's observation that, "Some situations are so bad, that to remain sane is insane."

What violence there may be among young people is no match for the accepted violence involved in a new kind of war; one which we cannot explain or justify on any valid grounds but which has killed over 40,000 men. Before we make any judgments about the illegal take-over of property and the inexcusable destruction of furniture, records and files that has occurred on college campuses, we ought to remember that the sense of life's sacredness, the demand for an end to this terrible war, has come from our young people. We worry about property; they worry about human life.

I am not a historian but I would wager a guess that never before in recorded human history has the younger generation been so concerned, so committed, so active, in the social issues of the times as this one. In a society as disease-ridden as ours, caught in the grip of the most vicious race prejudice, it is our *young* who understand what must be done in this land. There is among them a poignant and shimmering compassion for each other that totally disregards color. They are also the first generation of young people who see the impossibility of settling problems by war, they cannot be made blindly nationalistic by the waving of flags or the sound of marching bands, but they take their stand as members of the human family without concern for national boundaries.

The answer—if we are honest about it—is shocking to a tired parent's nervous system. The answer, my friends, is that *we wanted them this way!* If you think you can take it let's look back together to the early 1950s when we were the young and eager parents of this generation of teen-agers. What sorts of things did we begin to tell our children when

98

they were four or five or six? I know what *I* was saying—that war is terrible and that we had to find some better way to solve international problems; that people are the same all over the world—that there were good people and bad people in China, in Russia, and in the United States; and that most people want to live in peace and love. That it was a shame on our history and national honor that we treated Negroes and Indians, Mexican-Americans and Orientals, like second-class citizens and that our only salvation was a genuine belief in the brotherhood of man. That one shouldn't judge a person by how he looks or what he is wearing but what he *is* inside: that is, not to trust externals, but to be concerned with how a person lives his life with other people.

Weren't a great many of us saying that material possessions are unimportant, that what *is* important is the sacredness of life? Weren't we saying, don't judge a man by his credentials —his diploma, his insurance policies, the number of cars in his garage—judge him by what he does for other people? It seems to me that many of us were appalled in the 1950s by what Harold Taylor (then president of Sarah Lawrence College) called "The Understood Generation"—the young people of college age who seemed totally indifferent to the social stresses of McCarthyism and the Cold War and simply wanted that $40,000 house in the suburbs and the best investment plan for early retirement. We despaired over the conformist youth of that time, and we exhorted *our* children *not* to do likewise. "Get in there and *care!*" we said to them!

Now we look at the crazy costumes and the sandaled feet, and the fury at poverty and hate, and the refusal to be interested in neatness and order and getting one's union card for economic security—and we shudder. Can these be *our* children? The trouble was we weren't listening to ourselves. We were busy making money, getting comfortable, putting up with things as they are. But our children *did* listen, and I for one am proud of them.

*Teen-agers and Discipline*    Whatever conclusions one may come to about permissiveness and discipline it sure is a lot easier to put theory into practice when one's child is too young to really fight back.

One of the things that scares us about being the parents of teen-agers is that we feel we can no longer really punish effectively. Older children are away from home so much of the time that it is almost impossible to make punishment stick. You just can't hire a detective to follow teen-agers wherever they go. There comes a point where you just can't get away with yelling or spanking or isolating, and depriving a youngster just doesn't make any sense because you can't enforce it. Parents get a creepy feeling of helplessness. It's very scary to lose one's Parent Power!

Scary but inevitable. And because it is going to happen it behooves us to keep it in mind during those earlier years when we *do* have some leeway and control. In deciding on how to discipline a younger child we must keep in mind that today's teen-agers are not home very much and that they are far more influenced by their peers than by us. If this is so we ought to do everything possible to try to devise forms of discipline that will provide opportunities for learning the decision-making process—for the development of inner control based on a child's own successful evaluation of a situation.

We ought to remember that society has become so complex and turbulent that it is almost impossible to have an uneventful adolescence anymore. Our children understand this; they are not shocked by being arrested for example—something that we see as horrifying and shameful because it never happened to us. In one typical middle-class suburban family where the parents' only contact with the law was an occasional traffic ticket their fourteen-year-old son has twice been arrested. He has long hair and wears beads and one day he was waiting at a crossroads for his mother to pick him up and

* From *Natural Parenthood*. Pages 100–101, line 14.

drive him to a music lesson when a policeman told him to move on. He asked why, which strikes me as a reasonable question, and was taken to the police station for defying an officer.

Like it or not we have lost our total authority and responsibility where young people are concerned. It would seem, therefore, that one of the greatest contributions we could make toward a reasonably secure world for our kids would be to see to it that the community agencies with which they are likely to come in contact are enlightened—that they have an understanding of the stresses and strains of adolescence and the vision and compassion to provide the same kind of reasoned guidance *we* tried to bring to bear in the earlier years.

* *The Difference Is, They Tell Now*   A grandmother in her seventies summed up most succinctly a dilemma of today's parents of teen-agers when she observed, "When I married I was completely naïve and virginal; when my daughter married I *thought* she was a virgin; when my granddaughter marries the whole *world* will know that she's not!"

Times were changing rapidly when this Grandma's daughter was a young rebel of the nineteen-thirties and -forties; she was the first girl in the family to go to college and the first to live away from home before she married. Grandma *did* accept those newfangled ideas. But the one thing she did *not* have to face at that time, because no one told her anything about it, was her daughter's premarital sexual experience. She said, "I didn't know about that until two years ago when my daughter was trying to help me understand and accept what my granddaughter was doing. I was terribly shocked—all I could think was Thank God my daughter didn't let me know about herself at the time!"

Rapid change in ideas and behavior is not exactly new to our shook-up generation of middle-aged parents! What is

* From *Sex and Your Teen-ager*. Pages 101–103, line 15.

strikingly new is the degree to which our young people *show us* and *tell us,* very explicitly, what these changes are—what the sexual revolution is all about. We do not have the luxury of innocence, of being able to close our eyes and pretend that things are the way we would like them to be. Whatever we may try to do, whatever point of view we may develop, one thing seems clear; many of us are going to be confronted; we will not get off without committing ourselves to a point of view. There is no escape route!

Our children tell us how things are changing and they ask us to accept—even welcome—these changes. Many of us feel they are asking too much. Isn't it enough that we put up with change—do we have to give our blessing, too? As one father put it, in exasperation, "When I was 16, what I did behind the bushes on a warm summer night in the park was my own business. I let my parents sleep in blissful ignorance. Why can't my kid give me the same peace of mind? Instead he confronts me with 'A Moral Question'—should he or his girl friend pay for her pills—and if he pays should that item be included in his allowance!"

Of course there are still many young people who are secretive about their sexual attitudes and behavior. They tend to be the youngsters who have always had very limited communication with their parents—on this and many other subjects. What seems to be happening is that those of us who were most concerned about providing facts and values when our children were very young are merely getting exactly what we asked for! All along—ever since our children were four or five years old—we have been saying, "Let's talk. I want to help you figure things out. We'll talk about that when you're older." Our children took us at our word! If we feel we are being made to "face the music," it is exactly what we said we wanted!

In any event it seems clear that a great many of us are now being asked to participate quite directly and candidly in the decision-making processes that our older adolescents especially are going through, and because this is so we find ourselves very much in need of clarifying our own thinking. As one mother exclaimed, "This is a fine time for kids to insist that we examine our values! Just when everything is changing so fast, and there are no rules to guide us—that's the time they pick to force us to have opinions!"

One of the problems we have in trying to help our children make moral judgments in the area of heterosexual relations is that our children feel *we* aren't making very moral judgments about a great many other things, and they can't see much reason for listening to us about anything at all. It might be difficult to talk about moral sexual behavior with teenagers in Santa Barbara, California, when they see their beaches being destroyed by oil—put there for only one reason—human greed.

* *Homosexuality*  Two more highly publicized books on homosexuality have appeared recently to join the gathering mass of material on this subject. One book breaks with tradition and blames fathers for making homosexuals out of their sons, the other book sticks with the psychoanalytic catechism that it's all Mom's fault. I am disturbed by the fact that such books, expressing so little humility—so sure they know exactly what they are talking about—are likely to frighten a great many parents of young children and leave parents of homosexuals flooded with irreparable feelings of guilt. It seems to me that we are not in any position to be so sure about how parent-child relationships affect a child's sexual orientation.

Most psychiatric approaches to homosexuality have asserted that it is brought about during the first three or four years of life by the attitudes and behavior of one or both parents. There are a variety of descriptions of how parents behaved, but the judgments seem somewhat imprudent to me since I have never yet read or heard a case history without

* From *Natural Parenthood*. Pages 103–109, line 4.

being able to think of at least ten other families with similar characteristics where the boy children managed to become heterosexual males very nicely, thank you. Why some kids and not others? No analyst has ever answered this to my satisfaction or to that of a growing minority of psychologists and psychiatrists who are taking a new look at this subject.

Psychiatric theory to date has also assumed that homosexuality is pathological—that it is a disease. Before one accepts this assumption it seems reasonable to ask how come homosexuality was accepted so completely during some of the high moments in man's cultural history? If it is a disease why didn't it ruin these societies? There is general agreement that one of the proudest and most creative periods in human history occurred in Greece in about 456 B.C., when homosexuality was viewed as merely one of many acceptable ways to love.

The new breed of therapist asks not whether his patient is homosexual or heterosexual, but whether he has found successful avenues for expressing what is most special and valuable in himself as a human being. From such a point of view one's sexual preferences become secondary to other questions having to do with an individual's struggle to find his own identity as a person.

Undoubtedly one of the reasons that makes it so easy to view homosexuality as a disease is that, because of social attitudes, the majority of homosexuals seem to have more than their fair share of self-contempt and self-hatred. Anyone who grows up not liking himself is in trouble and in our society this is the likely fate of most homosexuals.

The danger is great that parents can become self-conscious and uneasy with their children when they read reports on how they influence their children's sexuality. I have seen mothers who are hysterical with fear when their perfectly normal four-year-old sons wanted to wear high heels, and affectionate fathers who are ashamed that they like to have their children climb into bed with them on Sunday morning. Have a little

104

humility! It isn't really that easy to influence a child's sexual orientation—even if it could be done it would take herculean efforts of day and night work by terribly determined people! It is important to remember that for every aggressively seductive mother and passive or emotionally absent father whose son turns out to be a homosexual, there are other mothers and fathers with exactly the same qualities who get to be grandmas and grandpas in the traditional fashion. If we do not yet understand the mysterious complexities involved it seems to me we have a responsibility not to offer inflexible theories to cover our ignorance.

The sensible parent will assume that a fulfilling and satisfying adult life must be based on self-acceptance and that, without concerning oneself with predicting future sexual preferences, the chances are good that a youngster who has a good image of himself is more than likely to become a heterosexual. At least we can say that such a child won't choose deviation or some degree of social separateness because of self-dislike. However, even in a relatively comfortable home, where parents enjoy their own sexuality and have encouraged their children to discover their own talents and possibilities a child may grow up to prefer homosexual relationships. Does that have to be the end of the world? I am reminded of an earlier day when a patrician mother discovered that her son wanted to be a truck driver and she said, "All right, if you must—but be the best truck driver you can be." The day may come when without feeling overwhelming panic and guilt a parent might be able to say, "Be a homosexual if you prefer, but be the best *person* who is a homosexual that you can possibly be."

*The Drug Problem*    It must come as no surprise to the Black community that now that most middle-class white families are being affected by the problems of teen-age drug addiction action is beginning to be taken by law enforcement agencies. There has been a 700 percent increase in drug-taking in the

105

high schools in the past five years, according to *Today's Children Magazine*. Black leaders have repeatedly made the point that if anybody can get whatever drug he wants, in any city, within a half hour, then somebody—a lot of somebodies—are very well aware of where it's coming from, but have not wanted to do anything about it. When Judges, and Mayors and Governors begin to see the infection spreading into their own homes then the problem that the poor have dealt with for years suddenly becomes worth a little concern.

What I fear now is that in this reaction there will be the usual simple-minded short-sighted approach we use when trying to solve most social problems. The indications are already there; dramatic raids of a few apartments, and a sudden willingness to spend money on propaganda programs in the schools on the dangers of drugs—but no inclination to change the quality of life that sends children in search of an escape from reality.

If we really want to face up to what the drug problem is all about I suggest that when you wake up tomorrow morning you keep a record of all the soul-destroying things you see and hear in the course of the day—and add to that, if you can, what you think it would be like to be a high-school student in one of today's cities. By the end of the day, if you are at all sensitive, you will be ready for a tranquilizer at least —*our* generation's answer to anxiety and despair.

*Roots and Wings*  Our daughter recently celebrated her eighteenth birthday and I found myself thinking of the profoundly wise comment of Hodding Carter, the liberal Southern newspaper editor, who said that the only things a parent can give a child are roots and wings. When the time comes to permit those wings to fly how we worry about whether or not the roots have been good enough!

It seems to me that for today's parents that process of letting go is especially tough for two reasons. The first reason is that we have arrived at a peculiar way of looking at our young

106

people. I would be willing to bet that almost every parent of an adolescent does exactly what I do; when I see evidence that the roots have been good, when I find something wonderful to celebrate and admire about the kind of human being my child has become, I think, "Well, that was just good luck." And, like every other parent, when there are indications that my child is less than perfect—that she too will have the struggles and strains of being human like all the rest of us—I am flooded with a sense of guilt—if I'd only done a better job as a parent I could have turned out a more flawless product.

This attitude is not merely ridiculous—let's face it—it's even a little paranoid! But acknowledging that doesn't make it go away, does it? We are a generation of parents who find it almost impossible to take credit for what is wonderful about our kids, but are in there shoving and pushing each other—vying for the position of Worst Parent of the Year! We seem to have learned to blame ourselves, quickly and loudly, as a kind of defense against letting anybody else do it first! And, it must be said in our defense, that there have been an awesome list of people, from J. Edgar Hoover down to the most recent author of the latest *How to Raise Your Child* book, who have had it in for us. However, before we continue this ritual of asking Freud's forgiveness for our sins, we might try coming to our senses!

The large majority of parents are decent people—no better and no worse than they are in the other roles they play in life as teachers, lawyers, bricklayers, salesmen and citizens—sometimes inspired, brilliant, dedicated, sometimes tired, impatient, dull-witted. As often as we could, we gave our very best, and as often as we could not help it, we gave our least and worst. That is the human condition and we are stuck with it. Under these circumstances we have every right to feel pleased and proud when we see evidence in our almost-adult children of sweetness, compassion, sensitivity and courage—if they've got it, it wasn't just luck. On the other hand it is neither necessary nor helpful to weep and wail and beat ourselves over the head because these same children can also seem irresponsible, thoughtless and just plain dumb, sometimes. Apparently a very simple thing has happened—they have turned out just like us—a mishmash of wonderful and terrible, delightful and awful, delicious and disgusting possibilities—they are, By God, *Human*—just like us!

When the time comes to let go, to see them take off, to trust the strength of their wings, we will be able to play this important part of parenthood far more effectively if we don't indulge in the self-pitying game of, "But I made so many mistakes—how can he fly?" What we have to repeat in a kind of exercise in good sense is something quite taken for granted by any intelligent mother bird, "The roots were the best I could provide—now the wings will have to get stronger through practice in flying." Our guilt feelings are strings attached to our children's wings—we had better relinquish them before we cripple the flyers.

The second reason we seem to run into difficulty when it is time to let go is that we are allergic to hostility! When our children come to the normal point in their development where they have to separate themselves from us one of their most important weapons is hate. What else will work?

And there we are—terrified, wounded—we wanted so much to be loved! We tried so hard to be lovable—how could a child of ours with all those years of orthodontia, all those expensive schools—and camps—all those long, understanding talks—how could he look at us with such defiance, such anger? It is the only way open to our children if they are to have any selfhood, the integrity of finding their own way.

If our young people are having a hard time growing to adulthood we had better look to the weapons we bring—our guilt, and our intolerance of being disliked. If we want to let our children go we had better stop feeling so sorry for our human fallibility, and we might try rejoicing in the courage it takes for our children to work up a healthy dislike so that they can start on their way! If we *really* let go—open-armed,

108

liking ourselves enough not to burden our children with our discomfort at being imperfect, those wings will bring them back for a visit now and then—and we will discover that they have become adults we can be proud of.

## TOPICS FOR PARENT MEETINGS
## AND DISCUSSIONS
## THE TEEN-AGE YEARS

The programs dealing with teen-agers on How Do Your Children Grow? were therefore given the following titles:

1. "Dad, do you think my girl friend or I should pay for the pill?"
   (Teen-agers often confront us now with attitudes and behavior that may have been just as true for an earlier generation but were then never shared with one's parents. How much honesty can we tolerate? When are our children asking for controls?)
2. "If I were a teen-age child, what would I think of me?"
   (Shifting roles with our children; do we really know what they are thinking and feeling—about themselves, or us?)
3. "When those anxious saints come marching, can we learn to live with them?"
   (The challenge our Youth present to us on the matter of living up to our professed convictions. Why today's young people so often seem in despair.)
4. "How do you feel about taking on *our* commitments, kids?"
   (The values, the hang-ups, the truths and the hypocrisies, of adult life today.)
5. " 'V' is for virginity."
   (Sex behavior and values of parents and their children. Changing morality? Are we clear on what we believe? How much help and direction do our young people want from us?)
6. "Hurrah for someone else's daughter's freedom!"
   (The degree to which parents find themselves caught in the

109

attitudes which they were taught as children: how hard it is to change.)
7. "I have this peculiar child who thinks marijuana is terrible." (Drugs, group pressures for conformity, parental attitudes.)
8. "Coward take my coward's hand."
(Importance of being able to tolerate and endure the anxiety and pain of today's young people. To offer our companionship and to have the courage to share in their pain.)

In general, parents of teen-agers talked about:

Loss of communication—embarrassment and awkwardness in talking with teen-age children, and they with parents.
Critical judgments of parents—often "right on target."
The necessary separation that must be accomplished during the adolescent years—through rebellion, through trying one's wings, and probably most of all, through making one's own mistakes.
The social issues which beset our Youth at every turn. Crisis is the natural order of things in their lives. The lack of social institutions that provide them with guidance or controls.
Radicalism, campus unrest, despair and hopelessness, cynicism.
Can we ask our children to carry the burdens of social change?
Aspects of adolescence that have changed or stayed the same—the social climate vs. psychological needs.
Social acceleration, pseudo-sophistication, the wish to be protected.
Parental attitudes towards pre-marital sex, homosexuality.
Learning to *let go*.

The sequence with which subjects were discussed was roughly this:

The feeling of Youth about the possibility of changing social institutions.
Is there a generation gap?
The meaning and cause of rebellion. The necessary separation struggle.

110

Problems of communication—keeping the lines of communication open.

Conflict with school authorities.

The importance of failure as a growing experience.

Rapid social change—affects on parents (language, clothing styles, music, hair styles, etc. Are parents being "radicalized" along with their children?)

Our compassion and sympathy for today's young people; is it shared by the majority of the population? Why are we afraid of today's young people? ("God, we have a beautiful generation!")

The quest for honesty, the unwillingness to settle for hypocrisy.

Sexual attitudes and behavior—what standards? What controls? Are values really changing?

The social revolution and its effects on young people.

Parental attempts to be open-minded but still to have convictions.

Parents as intermediaries with other adults who hate and fear young people.

The right to privacy of feelings.

Pressures on young people re co-ed dorms, freedom to make own choices—often too early. Peer pressures.

Affluence—the over-indulgence of young people.

Wanting our children to love us—fear of their hostility.

Parents' rights—respecting parents' feelings.

Need for emancipation, adventures, less supervision, need for risk-taking in the growth process.

Being able to endure a child's failures.

College pressures.

Helping our children accept the social challenges and find constructive outlets for their feelings of dismay and wish for change.

Suburban life and city life. Are they both "real"? Is suburbia an escape from real issues.

Do our children feel we worry too much, about too many things? Do they see us as over-protective.

Letting our feelings show. Expression of affection—saying it as we see it.

111

Dropping-out.

Need for radical changes in education, in the relevancy of curriculum. Need for innovation.

Helping Youth accept and live with imperfection. Where did they get the idea that life could be easy or fun?

The insanity and absurdity of life as they see it. Kent State. Vietnam. Pollution, over-population—the effect of the assassinations as they experienced them in their growing years.

The responsibility of parents to take action on social issues. Racial problems.

New life styles (communes, trial marriages, etc).

Sex education—confusion, misinformation, fantasy.

Drugs—legal problems, need for research, dangers of alcohol and cigarettes vs. marijuana. Vendetta against young people in the courts—amount of adult experimentation with drugs.

Profanity and Pornography. Parental attitudes.

Male and female roles—time of rapid change. Women's Lib.

Emphasis on cognitive development vs. concern re feelings.

Meaning of respect for parents.

Should young people behave differently with parents and with friends?

## SUPPLEMENTARY RESOURCES

*Plays For Parents of Teen-Agers*

*Going to Pot or Not* (on drugs). Socio-Guide-Dramas, Methods and Materials Press, 6 S. Derby Road, Springfield, New Jersey, 07081. Good short skits on many subjects, send for information re prices, etc.

*How Was the Trip?* (on drugs). Nat'l Institute for Mental Health, 5454 Wisconsin Ave., Chevy Chase, Maryland, 20015. Free scripts.

*Let's Get Basic* by Nora Stirling. Teen-age pressures, youth's concerns re morals, sex, academic achievement. Plays For Living, 44 E. 23rd St., New York, N.Y., 10010. Single copy, $2.00, packet of scripts, $12.00.

*The Man Nobody Saw* by Elizabeth Blake. White racism. Suggested by Kerner Commission report. Plays For Living.

*You Never Told Me* (on venereal disease). Bureau of Public Health Information, New York City Dept. of Health, 125 Worth St., New York, N.Y., 10003. Free scripts.

## Films For Parents of Teen-Agers

*Escape to Nowhere* 25 min., color, 1968. Sixteen-year-old girl living in drug culture. Professional Arts, Inc., P.O. Box 8484 Universal City, Calif. Rental, $27.50 for 3 days.

*Phoebe* McGraw-Hill. 28 min. Teen-age pregnancy and ambivalent feelings of the pregnant girl. Contemporary Films, 330 W. 42nd St. New York, N.Y. 10036. Rental, $8.00.

*Pull Down the House* TV newscaster Harry Reasoner and his teen-age son discussing the generation gap and trying to bridge it. 38 min. Association Films, 600 Grand Ave., Richfield, New Jersey, 07657. Rental, $20.00.

*Speedscene: The Problem of Amphetamine Abuse* 17 min., color, BFA Educational Media, 11559 Santa Monica Blvd., Los Angeles, Calif., 90025. Rental, $15.00.

## Monologues For Parents of Teen-Agers

*I'm a Man* by Judith Menken. Adolescent struggle for independence, parental anxieties and confusions about late hours, attitudes towards work, college, discipline. Nassau County Mental Health Association, 186 Clinton St., West Hempstead, New York. 50¢.

*The Date* by Judith Menken. Social life of teens, how much parental control? Same source and price.

*To Whom It May Concern* by Judith Menken. Sibling relations, leaving home, lack of communication. Same source and price.

*Why?* by Judith Menken. Mother discovers her daughter uses marijuana. Same source and price.

## Bibliography of Books and Pamphlets

*A Federal Sourcebook: Answers to the Most Frequently Asked Questions About Drugs* National Clearinghouse for Drug Abuse Information, 5454 Wisconsin Ave., Chevy Chase, Maryland, 20402. 25¢.

113

*Coming of Age in America* by Edgar Z. Friedenberg, Random House, 1965.

*Drug Abuse and Your Child* by Alice Shiller. Public Affairs Pamphelts, 381 Park Ave. S., New York, N.Y., 10016. 25¢.

*Growing Up Absurd* by Paul Goodman, Random House, 1960.

*Love and Sex in Plain Language* by Eric Johnson, Lippincott, 1965.

*The Uncommitted* by Kenneth Kenniston, Delta, 1965.

*The Vanishing Adolescent* by Edgar Z. Friedenberg. Beacon Press, 1960.

*Youth, Change and Challenge* by Erik Erikson, Basic Books, 1963.

# Chapter V

## IT HELPS TO TALK THINGS OVER

There was nothing accidental about our selection of group discussions as the format of "How Do Your Children Grow?" Why didn't we just present a series of lectures on childraising? Why didn't we bring together many experts to do the discussing among themselves?

Because of what we know about the ways in which learning takes place—both for children and adults, Dr. Dorothy Cohen, Professor of Education at the Bank Street College of Education, puts it this way, "The job is to teach children how to fish." By that she meant that if you have a hungry child you can feed him some fish—but after he's eaten what can he do the next time he's hungry? The job of the educator is to teach the hungry child *how to catch fish*. This is why I have been so discouraged by much of the current philosophy and practice in childhood education; we have taken intellectually hungry children and fed them thousands of facts. But we have rarely tried to help children find their own facts, find what they need to know, when they need to know it.

We really learn little or nothing from facts unless they are interwoven with our living experiences—unless they relate to our needs and motivations and most of all to our feelings. Facts become meaningful only as we experience them in "real life" and when a group of people sit down to talk with each

115

other—in a third grade classroom or on a television show about parenthood—that's when learning begins to take place —out of the living drama of real experiencing of ideas and feelings.

In organizing parent discussion groups the single most important factor is the choice of a leader. To the degree that it is possible to find well-trained professional leadership this is certainly desirable. An experienced social worker or psychologist or educator has a body of information that can be helpful in broadening the scope of the group's perspective, and is also aware of and skilled in handling some of the inevitable problems that emerge, such as the person who talks incessantly or the shy person who needs help in becoming part of the group, or sometimes helping an individual not to reveal more about himself or his family than he will feel comfortable about later on.

But in searching for leaders it seems to me to be of vital importance to be concerned about many factors other than professional degrees, years of experience and general professional status. By that last I mean that it may not necessarily be true that the chief psychiatrist of a local mental health clinic will be a better group leader than the Home Economics teacher in the local high school. Effective group leadership requires much more than knowledge of the subject and information about human dynamics. Some of the most brilliant clinicians make some of the worst group leaders! Whether or not one has the personality ingredients for group leadership seems to rest on many factors other than academic and work experiences. Here are a few of what seem to me to be the most essential characteristics to be sought for:

1. *Friendliness.* The leader must be a person who genuinely enjoys being with other people and feels a kind of exultation in their marvelous differences of background, personality, and ideas. The leader cannot like everyone—nobody can—but he can accept and respect every member of the group. He must believe that every member of the group has a

116

worthwhile contribution to make. Superficial friendliness never works—it's got to be the real thing.

2. *Emotional Maturity.* The most difficult task in group leadership is to find a happy balance between an open spontaneity and an irresponsible impulsivity. The leader who carefully watches every word he says, keeps the group from having a real and open experience with each other. For growth to take place we must take risks—we need the courage to be open and very much ourselves. It has always seemed to me that my first duty to the group is not to be careful in the sense of holding back my genuine ideas and feelings, and that if I am most truly myself I give everyone else the encouragement —the right—to do likewise. But that's only half the story; it is possible to misuse the concept of spontaneity—to say hurtful and irresponsible things—to make snap judgments that are invalid and unfair. A group leader must be able to temper his own reactions and handle difficult outbursts in the group.

3. *Listening Ability.* A lot of people listen but not so many really *hear!* Effective group leadership requires an ability to focus completely on what a person is saying and to hear not only the words but the music—the hidden inner feelings as they are reflected in the words. A parent may sigh deeply and say, "There are days when I'm sorry I ever had any children." If the leader only hears the words he misses the real message —which might very well be, "I am struggling terribly hard to accept all the different kinds of feelings so that I can be a better parent." A leader ought to feel free to make the fullest use of his special role—to provide ideas and information, to interpret, to insist on people giving each other a chance, etc.

4. *Self-Confidence.* There is probably nothing which throws more cold water on a group than to hear a leader say, "I've never done this sort of thing before and I'm scared to death," or "You know I usually work with individuals so you'll have to teach me the ropes here." Leadership requires a deep inner conviction that one has a genuine contribution to make and that one can live in reasonable comfort with the

117

unexpected, the unplanned-for. That doesn't mean feeling that one knows all the answers! It means accepting oneself fully as a person with both strengths and weaknesses, willing to gamble on the strengths.

5. *Sincerity and Intellectual Honesty.* The leader must "be himself" without affectation or pretense; he knows some things and he doesn't know a great many other things. He must never play games but must say what he feels and means with conviction—but never suggesting that his answers are necessarily anybody else's. He cannot attempt to solve all problems, to know all the answers, but he can always help the group to find the answers they are all seeking together. He tries to "teach them how to fish!"

6. *Skill in Leading a Discussion.* One of the most important functions of leadership is the ability to guide discussion so that important points and aspects of the topic under discussion are covered. Even if a particular point is important and the argument interesting the leader may have to help the group clarify and return to its major aims and goals, lest they lose their sense of direction in concentrating too long on one point. Occasional brief summarizing of the discussion can sometimes be helpful. As part of his skill in leading the discussion a leader must have some plan for each meeting, no matter how vague, sketchy and flexible this may be.

These are crucial issues to evaluate in the selection of both a professional and a non-professional group leader. And as far as I am concerned it is impossible to make value judgments about good leadership strictly on the basis of professional training. I have seen some of the most eminent figures in psychology do disastrous things in parents' groups, and I have seen lay-leaders who are wonderfully sensitive and wise in their relations with a group. Each has its place and can be effective. When using non- or semi-professional leaders it seems to me that one has to be more aware of the need for consultation services and other community resources. The responsible lay-leader gets as much information and training

118

as can be found, provides a variety of books, expressing different points of view, uses mental health films and plays occasionally, and has regular consultations with someone in the community who is trained in one of the mental health disciplines.

*Helping Children Grow*    I have tried to provide you with food for thought—ideas that you must feel free to select and juggle and re-assemble and discard in the light of your own needs and feelings and experiences.

But it seems to me that in order to *be* most individualistically selective one must know a good deal about oneself and it is my hope that you have watched a search, and have joined it—that you are perhaps more prepared to have the courage to look within, to assess your own feelings, to examine your own ideas.

For I believe that the heart of growing as a parent is not using other people's ideas about child-development, but self-discovery, growing as an adult person, becoming so sensitized to one's own inner child of Being, that one comes to "naturally" understand and empathize with what a child feels and needs.

I suppose if I had to characterize a parent discussion group, it would be a meeting of gardeners trying to learn more about growing things. For in essence parenting is gardening.

This doesn't mean that a gardener just sits by and watches —permissively! He prunes the ivy; he thins the plants when they are coming in too thickly to grow well; he ties a climbing, wandering stem to a stick or a wall to make it grow upward. But he *never* says, "If I feed you and care for you and love you, you must grow exactly as I tell you to."

What makes the great gardener is his sense of wonder and delight and his command only that his plants be most alive and wondrously themselves, so that he can exult in the mysterious marvels of nature's great gifts.

Happy Gardening!

# AGENCIES, SERVICES, AND RESOURCES

While it has been our hope that these programs outlined can be used in parent groups as a springboard for further discussion, it will also be helpful for such groups to have at their disposal a broad variety of other resources for stimulating discussion.

The best and most all-encompassing agency that I know about is The Mental Health Materials Center at 419 Park Ave. S., New York, N.Y. 10016, Executive Director, Mr. Alex Sareyan. This is an organization that publishes mental health materials for a number of social-community agencies, and is therefore in a position to know a good deal about the latest and the best that are available. In addition it provides a special subscription service for community agencies called The Information Resources Center. The subscription charge is $100.00 for the first year and $50.00 thereafter—which may sound quite steep but the service is remarkable and unique. It seems to me that any community organization that really wants to bring to the attention of its members, or the general public, the latest and best information and programs in the mental health field, cannot afford to do without this service. Interested groups could certainly recommend that the service ought, at least, to be made available through one's local public library or Mental Health Association.

This subscription service provides literally hundreds of bulletins each year reporting on and evaluating books, pamphlets, plays and films in the mental health field. The committee that reviews all these materials is made up of knowledgeable professional people working in mental health, and I have found its recommendations sound and extremely helpful— and am deeply indebted to IRC and Mr. Sareyan for much of the reference material in this book.

Another excellent service that I have found enormously helpful is The Nassau County Mental Health Association,

186 Clinton St., West Hempstead, New York, Executive Director, Mrs. Betty Jones. If you live in the New York area, this agency puts on a yearly "Showcase of Mental Health Materials" that is invaluable to program planners. This is also the agency that publishes all the Monologues, already listed in Chapters Two, Three and Four. I have already introduced the Monologues in Chapter Two, but must add here that I have never used a Monologue in either a large PTA meeting or a small study group without finding that this simple short presentation stimulated immediate and inspired discussion.

Probably the oldest organization involved in parent education program planning is The Child Study Association of America, 9 E. 89th St., New York, N.Y. 10028, Executive Director, Mr. James Ottenberg. They have an excellent list of publications for parents and educators and if you are in the New York area, they also provide direct service in counseling organizations about setting up study group programs and obtaining good leadership for them. They publish a pamphlet that is very useful to program planners and group leaders entitled, *When Parents Get Together* (booklet #716, $1.00).

Chapters Two, Three and Four also list a number of excellent mental health plays. Many of them come from *Plays For Living*, Family Service Association of America, 44 E. 23rd St., New York, N.Y., 10010. The person to contact for information about performance arrangements or purchase of scripts is Mrs. Ann Booth. Within a radius of 50-miles of New York City arrangements can be made to have a professional company of actors perform the plays; in fact, within this area, this is required for some of the plays. The cost is $85.00 plus transportation for the cast. What is frequently done is that several groups will join forces for a meeting and share the costs.

A useful source of short skits on a wide range of mental health subjects is "Socio-Guide-Dramas." Information about

121

subjects covered and purchase of scripts is available by writing to: Methods and Materials Press, 6 South Derby Road, Springfield, New Jersey, 07081.

A useful and quite comprehensive list of mental health pamphlets comes from Public Affairs Pamphlets, 381 Park Ave. S., New York, N.Y., 10016, Editor, Mrs. Adele Braude. The pamphlets are all 25¢ each, with lower prices for quanity purchase.

There is an organization in New York that provides first-rate information about youth in general, and drug problems in particular. Two Newsletters are published monthly. One is called *Addiction and Drug Abuse Report*. It is a well informed guide to the latest research, the most helpful community programs, and an excellent general discussion of the issues involved in this urgent and distressing problem. The second Newsletter, *Youth Report,* gives a variety of useful information about teen-agers in general; what they are thinking and feeling, their problems and conflicts, their goals and hopes, community services for youth, their social concerns— and who is doing what to improve our understanding of the world as our adolescents view it. Both Newsletters are published by Grafton Publications, Inc., 331 Madison Ave., New York, N.Y., 10017, Mr. Samuel Grafton, Editor. Subscription rate for each Newsletter is $18.00 a year.

Another source of information on drug problems is The National Clearing House For Drug Abuse Information, 5454 Wisconsin Ave., Chevy Chase, Maryland, 20015.

The Sex Information and Education Council of the United States, 1855 Broadway, New York, N.Y. 10019, Executive Director, Dr. Mary Calderone, provides excellent, knowledgeable resource materials on sex education program planning and general information about sexual development, marriage and family living.

The American Social Health Association, 1790 Broadway, New York, N.Y., 10019, Executive Director, Mrs. Elizabeth

122

Force, is another excellent source of guidance in program planning for mental health education.

Through its Children's Bureau, The U.S. Dept. of Health, Education and Welfare provides a mass of helpful mental health materials of all kinds. Another governmental source of assistance is The National Institute of Mental Health, 5454 Wisconsin Ave., Chevy Chase, Maryland, 20015.

The main headquarters of the National Parent-Teacher Association, 700 N. Rush St., Chicago, Ill., 60611, is well known to most parents as a never-ending source of study guides and reference materials that are easily accessible through state and local branches. Every issue of the PTA Magazine provides outlines for group discussion of a very wide variety of articles.

The National Association for Mental Health, 10 Columbus Circle, New York, N.Y., 10019, and all its affiliate branches all over the country, are an obvious and good source of information.

The National Council of Churches of Christ in America, 475 Riverside Drive, New York, N.Y., has had an active and very good Family Life Department for many years, providing literature and direct educational services.

Human Relations Aids is another arm of The Mental Health Materials Center, 419 Park Ave. S., New York, N.Y., 10016. This agency publishes an excellent pamphlet by Dr. Nina Ridenour entitled, *Memorandum to Discussion Leaders,* 25¢ each. It offers basic principles and practical suggestions to group leaders.

In Chapters Two, Three and Four there are lists of useful films to be used as a springboard to group discussion. Here are some of the places from which they and many other films can be rented:

Campus Film Distributors Corp., 14 E. 53rd St., New York, N.Y., 10022.

Contemporary Films, 330 W. 42nd St., New York, N.Y., 10036.

Encyclopaedia Britannica Films, 202 E. 44th St., New York, N.Y.

International Film Bureau, 332 S. Michigan Ave., Chicago, Ill., 60604.

Mental Health Film Board, 116 E. 38th St., New York, N.Y., 10016.

Mental Health Materials Center, 419 Park Ave. S., New York, N.Y. 10016.

National Association for Mental Health, 10 Columbus Circle, New York, N.Y., 10019.

National Film Board of Canada, 680 Fifth Ave., New York, N.Y., 10019.

New York University Film Library, 29 Washington Square, New York, N.Y.

Many of these organizations can supply film bibliographies. Two useful bibliographies are:

*Selected Mental Health Films.* Public Health Service Publication no. 1591, U.S. Government Printing Office, Washington, D.C. 20402. 40¢.

*Selected Films on Child Life.* Children's Bureau Publication, no. 376, same address and price as above.